Crisis and Escalation in Cyberspace

Martin C. Libicki

Prepared for the United States Air Force

PROJECT AIR FORCE

The research described in this report was sponsored by the United States Air Force under Contract FA7014-06-C-0001. Further information may be obtained from the Strategic Planning Division, Directorate of Plans, Hq USAF.

Library of Congress Cataloging-in-Publication Data is available for this publication.

ISBN: 978-0-8330-7678-6

The RAND Corporation is a nonprofit institution that helps improve policy and decisionmaking through research and analysis. RAND's publications do not necessarily reflect the opinions of its research clients and sponsors.

RAND® is a registered trademark.

Published 2012 by the RAND Corporation
1776 Main Street, P.O. Box 2138, Santa Monica, CA 90407-2138
1200 South Hayes Street, Arlington, VA 22202-5050
4570 Fifth Avenue, Suite 600, Pittsburgh, PA 15213-2665
RAND URL: http://www.rand.org/
To order RAND documents or to obtain additional information, contact
Distribution Services: Telephone: (310) 451-7002;
Fax: (310) 451-6915; Email: order@rand.org

Preface

This report presents some of the results of a fiscal year 2011 RAND Project AIR FORCE study on the integration of kinetic and nonkinetic weapons, "U.S. and Threat Non-Kinetic Capabilities." It discusses the management of cybercrises throughout the spectrum from precrisis to crisis to conflict.

The basic message is simple: Crisis and escalation in cyberspace can be managed as long as policymakers understand the key differences between nonkinetic conflict in cyberspace and kinetic conflict in the physical world. Among these differences are the tremendous scope that cyberdefense affords; the near impossibility and thus the pointlessness of trying to disarm an adversary's ability to carry out cyberwar; and the great ambiguity associated with cyberoperations—notably, the broad disjunction between the attacker's intent, the actual effect, and the target's perception of what happened. Thus, strategies should concentrate on (1) recognizing that crisis instability in cyberspace arises largely from misperception, (2) promulgating norms that might modulate crisis reactions, (3) knowing when and how to defuse inadvertent crises stemming from incidents, (4) supporting actions with narrative rather than signaling, (5) bolstering defenses to the point at which potential adversaries no longer believe that cyberattacks (penetrating and disrupting or corrupting information systems, as opposed to cyberespionage) can alter the balance of forces, and (6) calibrating the use of offensive cyberoperations with an assessment of their escalation potential.

The research reported here was sponsored by Gen Gary North, Commander, U.S. Pacific Air Forces, and conducted within the Force Modernization and Employment Program of RAND Project AIR FORCE. It should be of interest to the decisionmakers and policy researchers associated with cyberwarfare, as well as to the Air Force strategy community.

RAND Project AIR FORCE

RAND Project AIR FORCE (PAF), a division of the RAND Corporation, is the U.S. Air Force's federally funded research and development center for studies and analyses. PAF provides the Air Force with independent analyses of policy alternatives affecting the development, employment, combat readiness, and support of current and future air, space, and cyber forces. Research is conducted in four programs: Force Modernization and Employment; Manpower, Personnel, and Training; Resource Management; and Strategy and Doctrine.

Additional information about PAF is available on our website: http://www.rand.org/paf/

Contents

Preface iii
Figures and Table ix
Summary xi
Acknowledgments xxiii
Abbreviations xxv

CHAPTER ONE
Introduction 1
Some Hypothetical Crises 2
Mutual Mistrust Is Likely to Characterize a Cybercrisis 5
States May Have Room for Maneuver in a Cybercrisis 10
A Note on Methodology 16
Purpose and Organization 17

CHAPTER TWO
Avoiding Crises by Creating Norms 19
What Kind of Norms Might Be Useful? 20
  Enforce Laws Against Hacking 20
  Dissociate from Freelance Hackers 22
  Discourage Commercial Espionage 23
  Be Careful About the Obligation to Suppress Cybertraffic 24
How Do We Enforce Norms? 24
Confidence-Building Measures 26
Norms for Victims of Cyberattacks 28
Norms for War 29
  Deception 30

Military Necessity and Collateral Damage 31
Proportionality 33
Reversibility 35
Conclusions 36

CHAPTER THREE
Narratives, Dialogue, and Signals 39
Narratives to Promote Control 40
A Narrative Framework for Cyberspace 41
Victimization, Attribution, Retaliation, and Aggression 44
    Victimization 45
    Attribution 46
    Retaliation 47
    Aggression 49
Emollients: Narratives to Walk Back a Crisis 50
    "We Did Nothing" 51
    "Well, At Least Not on Our Orders" 54
    "It Was an Accident" 57
    "This Is Nothing New" 58
    "At Least It Does Not Portend Anything" 60
    Broader Considerations 61
Signals 62
    Ambiguity in Signaling 65
    Signaling Resolve 67
    Signaling That Cybercombat Is Not Kinetic Combat 69
Conclusions 70

CHAPTER FOUR
Escalation Management 73
Motives for Escalation 74
    Does Escalation Matter? 76
Escalation Risks 78
    Escalation Risks in Phase 0 78
    Escalation Risks for Contained Local Conflicts 80
    Escalation Risks for Uncontained Conflicts 81
Managing Proxy Cyberattacks 84

What Hidden Combatants Imply for Horizontal Escalation............. 84
Managing Overt Proxy Conflict................................. 88
The Difficulties of Tit-for-Tat Management........................ 89
The Importance of Preplanning............................. 90
Disjunctions Among Effort, Effect, and Perception 91
Inadvertent Escalation.................................... 93
Escalation into Kinetic Warfare............................... 97
Escalation into Economic Warfare............................ 99
Sub-Rosa Escalation 103
Managing the Third-Party Problem 106
The Need for a Clean Shot................................... 108
Inference and Narrative 110
Command and Control 114
Commanders 114
Those They Command 117
Conclusions.. 120

CHAPTER FIVE
Implications for Strategic Stability........................... 123
Translating Sources of Cold War Instability to Cyberspace 123
What Influence Can Cyberwar Have If Nuclear Weapons Exist? 124
Can a Cyberattack Disarm a Target State's Nuclear Capabilities? 125
Can a Cyberattack Disarm a Target State's Cyberwarriors? 126
Does Cyberwar Lend Itself to Alert-Reaction Cycles? 129
Are Cyberdefenses Inherently Destabilizing?.................... 129
Would a Cyberspace Arms Race Be Destabilizing?...................... 130
Surprise Attack as a Source of Instability 133
Misperception as a Source of Crisis........................... 135
One Side Takes Great Exception to Cyberespionage 136
Defenses Are Misinterpreted as Preparations for War.................... 136
Too Much Confidence in Attribution........................... 138
Too Much Confidence in or Fear of Preemption 139
Supposedly Risk-Free Cyberattacks........................... 141
Neutrality.. 143
Conclusions.. 144

CHAPTER SIX
Can Cybercrises Be Managed? 147

APPENDIXES
A. **Distributed Denial-of-Service Attacks** 151
B. **Overt, Obvious, and Covert Cyberattacks and Responses** 155
C. **Can Good Cyberdefenses Discourage Attacks?** 159

Bibliography 163

Figures and Table

Figures

3.1. Alternative Postures for a Master Cyber Narrative 43
4.1. Sources of Imprecision in Tit for Tat 76
4.2. An Inadvertent Path to Mutual Escalation 94
A.1. Configuring Networks to Limit the Damage of
Distributed Denial-of-Service Attacks 153

Table

B.1. Overt, Obvious, and Covert Cyberattacks and Responses ... 155

Summary

Background

The chances are growing that the United States will find itself in a cybercrisis—the escalation of tensions associated with a major cyber-attack, suspicions that one has taken place, or fears that it might do so soon. By *crisis*, we mean an event or events that force a state to take action in a relatively short period of time or face the fraught consequences of inaction. When they fear that failure to act leads to war or a great loss of standing, states believe they must quickly decide whether to act.[1] When we use the term *cyberattacks*, we refer to what may be a series of events that start when systems are penetrated and may culminate in such events as blackouts, scrambled bank records, or interference with military operations.

The basis for such a forecast is twofold. First, the reported level of cyberincidents (most of which are crimes or acts of espionage) continues to rise. Second, the risks arising from cyberspace are perceived as growing more consequential, perhaps even faster.

---

[1] Richard Ned Lebow, *Between Peace and War: The Nature of International Crisis*, Baltimore, Md.: Johns Hopkins University Press, 1981, pp. 7–12, has a good discussion of the definition of *crisis*.

Purpose

The genesis for this work was the broader issue of how the Air Force should integrate kinetic and nonkinetic—that is, cyber—operations.[2] Central to this process was careful consideration of how escalation options and risks should be treated, which, in turn, demanded a broader consideration across the entire crisis-management spectrum.

To put the material on escalation into a broader context, we preface it with an examination of appropriate norms for international conduct with a focus on modulating day-to-day computer-network exploitation and building international confidence (Chapter Two). Chapter Three covers narratives, dialogue, and signals: what states can and should say about cybercrises. A state that would prevail has to make a clear story with good guys and bad guys without greatly distorting the facts (beyond their normal plasticity).

Chapter Four broaches the subject of limiting an open conflict. If cyberwarfare is clearly subordinate to violent combat (both in the sense that it is overshadowed by violent conflict and in the sense that it can be instrumental to violent conflict while the reverse is much less likely to be true), then the control of the latter is likely to dominate the former. But if cyberwar takes place without violent accompaniment or if the effects of cyberattack are global while the violence is local, then the management of cyberconflict becomes more important.

The penultimate chapter then builds from that material to discusses strategic stability. Primarily, it argues that crises are less likely to emanate from the unavoidable features of cyberspace than they are to arise from each side's fear, putatively exaggerated, of what may result from its failure to respond. Chapter Six asks and answers the question whether cybercrises can be managed.

---

[2]   Nonkinetic operations can also be other than cyber, such as psychological or information operations, but the study team focused on cyber.

Avoiding Crises by Creating Norms

Norms—accepted standards of behavior—can help avert crises arising from misperception, mistakes, or misattribution. Obligations to assist investigations of cyberattacks, when met, can help build mutual confidence. Those that persuade states to dissociate themselves from nonstate hackers can make it harder for targets of cyberattack to accuse a given state of being complicit in what might have been criminal attacks. Renouncing espionage to steal intellectual property can help reduce certain tensions associated with the frictions of international trade. But norms are no panacea: Some of what the United States might ask others to do—such as control the bots that spew spam to the rest of the world—are difficult for the United States itself to do.

Norms to govern state behavior in peacetime may be useful even if unenforceable. They put nations on record against certain behaviors. Even if states sign up while harboring reservations or maintaining a cynical determination not to comply, others—such as a nation's own citizens or whistleblowers who balk when asked to act contrarily to norms—may be there to remind states to obey the constraints to which they agreed.

Norms that govern the use of cyberattacks in wartime may also be useful, but enthusiasm about their beneficial effect should be tempered. A state can vow to limit its attacks to military targets, react proportionally to provocation, and avoid deception only to find out that the poor correspondence between intent and effect (and perception) in cyberspace means that it did no such thing.

Narratives, Dialogues, and Signaling

The inherently secret, often incomprehensible, and frequently ambiguous nature of cyberoperations suggests that what actually happened can be overshadowed by the narratives that are used to explain events—especially if the focus on cyberevents is not overwhelmed by the subsequent violence of war. Narratives are made up of the stories that people, organizations, and states tell about themselves to others as a way of putting events in a broader and consistent context and justifying their attitudes and actions.

Conflicts, to be sure, have always needed explanation, but perhaps nowhere more so than for cyberwar. Cyberoperations lack much precedent or much expressed declared policy on which to rely. The normal human intuition about how things work in the physical world does not always translate effectively into cyberspace. Finally, the effects, and sometimes even the fact, of cyberoperations can be obscure. The source of the attacks may not be obvious. The attacker must claim them, or the defender must attribute them. Even if the facts were clear, their interpretations are not; even when both are clear, decisionmakers and opinionmakers may not necessarily understand.

Today, the level of cyber knowledge, much less expertise, in governments is quite low. This will change, but only slowly. As people gain savvy about cyberspace, narratives about incidents necessarily must become more sophisticated and nuanced. Until then, states, nonstate actors, and partisans on all sides have a great opportunity to make something of nothing or vice versa. If cyberwar becomes more consequential, look for states to avail themselves of such opportunities more often. Narratives become tools of crisis management.

Part of the strategy of interpretation is concocting narratives in which events take their designated place in the logical and moral scheme of things: We are good, you are bad; we are strong and competent, unless we have stumbled temporarily because of your evil. Alternatively, the emphasis can be on systems: how complex they are, how easily they fall victim to accident or malice, the difficulty of determining what happened to them, the need to reassert competence, the importance of one network's or system's stability to the stability of all networks and systems. Within wide bands of plausibility, narratives are what states choose to make them.

Dialogue may be needed to manage crises in which incidents arise unrelated to ostensible military or strategic moves by the alleged attacker: If the attribution is correct, what was the motive? The accused state may, alternatively or sequentially, claim that it was innocent, that the attackers did not work at the state's behest (even if they are state employees), that the incident was an accident, that it was nothing unprecedented, or that it really signified nothing larger than what it was. The accusing state (that is, the victim of the cyberattack) may reject these claims, find a way to verify them (e.g., if the accused state dissociates itself from the attackers, is it also prepared to act against them?), or conclude that it must live with what happened. In some cases, one state takes actions that are within the bounds of what it thinks it can do, only to find that its actions are misread, misinterpreted, or taken to be a signal that the other state never intended to send. Key to this analysis is each side's perception of what the incidents in question were trying to achieve or signal (if anything).

Signals, by contrast with narratives, supplant or supplement words with deeds—often, indications that one or another event is taken seriously and has or would have repercussions. Signaling is directed communication, in contrast with narratives, which are meant for all. Signals gain seriousness by indicating that a state is taking pains to do something; costliness gives signals credibility.

Signals, unfortunately, can be as or more ambiguous when they take place or refer to events in cyberspace than they are when limited to the physical world. For example, the United States recently established U.S. Cyber Command. What might this convey? It could signal that the United States is prepared. It could also signal that it is afraid of what could happen to its own systems. Alternatively, it could signal that it is going to be more aggressive. Or it could indicate some combination of those things. Hence the role of narratives—such as one that emphasizes, for instance, that a particular state is fastidious about rule of law. They are an important complement to signals and perhaps an alternative or a substitute way for others to understand and predict a state's actions.

Escalation Management

Possibilities for escalation management, once conflicts start, must assume that quarreling states would prefer less disruption and violence versus more of it—once they make their points to each other.

The escalation risks from one side's cyberoperations depend on how the other side views them. Because phase 0 operations—preparing the cyberbattlefield by examining potential targets and implanting malware in them or bolstering defenses—tend to be invisible, they should carry little risk. Yet, if they are revealed or discovered, such actions may allow the other side to draw inferences about what those that carried them out are contemplating. Operational cyberwar against targets that are or could be hit by kinetic attacks ought to be unproblematic—unless the other side deems cyberattacks particularly heinous or prefatory to more-expansive attacks on homeland targets. Strategic cyberwar might well likely become a contest of competitive pain-making and pain-taking that is inherently escalatory in form—even if no kinetic combat is taking place.

Tit-for-tat strategies can often be a way to manage the other side's escalation: "If you cross this line, so will I, and then you will be sorry." However, in the fog of cyberwar, will it be obvious when a line is crossed? As noted, the linkages between intent, effect, and perception are loose in cyberspace. Furthermore, if lines are not mutually understood, each side may climb up the proverbial escalation ladder certain that it crossed no lines but believing that the other side did. Assumptions that each side must respond at the speed of light could exacerbate both sides' worst tendencies. In reality, if neither side can disarm the other, then each can take its time deciding how to influence the other.

Third-party participation may well be a feature of cyberspace because the basic tools are widespread, geographical distance is nearly irrelevant, and the odds of being caught may be too low to discourage mischief. A problematic third party might be a powerful friend of a rogue state that the United States is confronting. If the powerful friend carries out cyberattacks against U.S. forces or interests, the United States would have to consider the usefulness of responding to such attacks. Even in symmetric conflicts, the possibility of third-party attacks should also lend caution to responses to escalation that look as if they came from the adversary but may not have. Because escalation management entails anticipating how the other side will react to one's actions, there is no substitute for careful and nuanced understanding of other states. Local commanders are more likely than remote ones to have such understanding; paradoxically, however, the former do not currently exercise much command and control (C2) over cyberwarriors.

Strategic Stability

With all these concerns about managing cybercrises, it may be worthwhile here to step back and ask whether the existence or at least possibility of cyberwar threatens strategic stability. The best answer is both no and yes: no in that the acts that make nuclear instability an issue do not carry over to cyberspace (attacks meant to temporarily confound conventional forces, as noted, aside), and yes in that other factors lend instability to the threat of the use of cyberwar.

Why the no? First, nuclear weapons themselves limit the existential consequences of any cyberattack. A nuclear-armed state (or its allies) might yield to the will of another state, but it cannot be taken over except at a cost that far outweighs any toll a cyberattack could exact. Cyberattacks cannot cause a state's nuclear weapons to disappear (Stuxnet merely slowed Iran's attempts to build one), and, although cyberattacks could, in theory, confound nuclear C2, nuclear states tend to bulletproof their C2. Attackers may find it hard to be sufficiently confident that they have disabled all forms of adversary nuclear C2 to the point at which they can then act with impunity.

Equally important is the fact that no state can disarm another's cybercapabilities through cyberwar alone. Waging cyberwar takes only computers, access to the Internet, some clever hackers, and intelligence on the target's vulnerabilities sufficient to create exploits. It is hard to imagine a first strike that could eliminate all (or perhaps even any) of these capabilities. If a first strike cannot disarm and most effects induced by a cyberattack are temporary, is it really that destabilizing?

Furthermore, cyberconflict does not lend itself to a series of tit-for-tat increases in readiness. During the Cold War, an increase in the readiness of nuclear forces on one side prompted a similar response from the other, and so on. This follows because raising the alert level is the primary response available, the advantage of the first strike is great, and preparations are visible. None of this applies to cyberwar, in which many options are available, what happens tends not to be visible, and first strikes cannot disarm. In addition, during the Cold War, making nuclear strike capabilities invulnerable was perceived as enormously destabilizing because it rendered the opponent's nuclear arsenal harmless by destroying it. But, in large part because cyberdefenses will never be perfect, they pose no such threat and thus are not inherently destabilizing.

Arms races have traditionally fostered instability. Such a race already exists in cyberspace between offense and defense. Offense-offense races are less plausible. There is no compelling reason to develop an offensive weapon simply because a potential adversary has one. It is hard to know what others have, and the best response to an offensive cyberweapon is to fix the vulnerabilities in one's own system that allow such cyberweapons to work.

However, the subjective factors of cyberwar do pave paths to inadvertent conflict. Uncertainties about allowable behavior, misunderstanding defensive preparations as offensive ones, errors in attribution, unwarranted confidence that cyberattacks are low risk because they are hard to attribute, and misunderstanding the norms of neutrality are all potentially sources of instability and crisis. Examples can include the following:

- Computer network exploitation—espionage, in short—can foster misperceptions and possibly conflict. Normally, espionage is not seen as a reason to go to war. Everyone spies on everyone, even allies. But then one side tires of having its networks penetrated; perhaps the frequency and volume of exploitation crosses some unclear red line; or the hackers simply make a mistake tampering with systems to see how they work and unintentionally damage something.
- One side's defensive preparations could give the other side the notion that its adversary is preparing for war. Or preparing offensive capabilities for possible eventual use could be perceived as an imminent attack. Because much of what goes on in cyberspace is invisible, what one state perceives as normal operating procedure, another could perceive as just about anything.

- The difficulties of attribution can muddle an already confused situation. Knowing who actually did something in cyberspace can be quite difficult. The fact that numerous attacks can be traced to the servers of a specific country does not mean that that state launched the attack or even that it originated in that country. Or, even if it did originate there, that fact does not mean that the state is complicit. It could have been launched by a cybercriminal cartel that took over local servers. Or some third party could have wanted it to look as though a state launched an attack.

Cyberwar also provides rogue militaries with yet another way to carry out a no-warning attack, another potential source of instability. If an attacker convinces itself that its efforts in cyberspace cannot be traced back to it, the attacker may view an opening cyberattack as a low-risk proposition: If it works well enough, the attacker can follow up with kinetic attacks, and, if it fails to shift the balance of forces sufficiently, no one will be the wiser. If the attacker is wrong about its invisibility, however, war or at least crisis may commence.

Otherwise, from a purely objective perspective, cyberwar should not lead to strategic instability. However, cyberwar may not be seen as it actually is, and states may react out of fear rather than observation and calculation. An action that one side perceives as innocuous may be seen as nefarious by the other. A covert penetration may be discovered and require explanation. Cyberwar engenders worry. There is little track record of what it can and cannot do. Attribution is difficult, and the difficulties can tempt some while the failure to appreciate such difficulties can tempt others. Espionage, crime, and attack look very similar. Nonstate actors can pose as states. Everything is done in secret, so what one state does must be inferred and interpreted by others. Fortunately, mistakes in cyberspace do not have the potential for catastrophe that mistakes do in the nuclear arena. Unfortunately, that fact may lead people to ignore the role of uncertainty and doubt in assessing the risk of inadvertent crisis.

Conclusions and Recommendations for the Air Force

Cybercrises can be managed by taking steps to reduce the incentives for other states to step into crisis, by controlling the narrative, understanding the stability parameters of the crises, and trying to manage escalation if conflicts arise from crises. Given the paucity of cyberwar to date, our analysis produces more suggestions than recommendations. That noted, an essential first step of cybercrises is to recognize them for what they are, rather than metaphors of what they could be.

As for recommendations, the Air Force can contribute a great deal to assist in cybercrisis management:

- Crisis stability suggests that the Air Force find ways of conveying to others that its missions can be carried out in the face of a full-fledged cyberattack, lest adversaries come to believe that a large-scale no-warning cyberattack can provide a limited but sufficient window of vulnerability to permit kinetic operations.
- The Air Force needs to carefully watch the messages it sends out about its operations, both explicit (e.g., statements) and implicit. To be sure, cyberspace, in contrast to the physical domains, is an indoor and not an outdoor arena. It may thus be hard to predict what others will see about offensive Air Force operations in cyberspace, much less how they might read it. But the assumption that unclassified networks are penetrated and thus being read by potential adversaries may be a prudent, if pessimistic, guide to how potential adversaries may make inferences about Air Force capabilities and intentions.
- If there is a master narrative about any such cybercrisis, it is axiomatic that Air Force operations should support rather than contradict such a narrative. The Air Force should, in this regard, consider how cyberspace plays in the Air Force's own master narrative as a source of potentially innovative alternatives—wisely selected and harvested—to meet military and national security objectives.
- The Air Force should clearly differentiate between cyberwar operations that can be subsumed under kinetic operations and cyberwar operations that cannot be subsumed. The former are unlikely

to be escalatory (although much depends on how such options are perceived) when their effects are less hazardous than a kinetic alternative would be. The latter, however, may create effects that could not be achieved by kinetic operations that, if undertaken, would be universally perceived as escalatory.

- Finally, Air Force planners need a precise understanding of how their potential adversaries would perceive the escalatory aspect of potential offensive operations. Again, more work, with particular attention to specific foes, is warranted. For this purpose (and for many others), the Air Force should develop itself as an independent source of expertise on cyberwar.

Acknowledgments

RAND work profits enormously from helpful hands and helpful hints. This monograph is no exception, and many individuals deserve heartfelt acknowledgments. First is the RAND team that worked on the overall project. Its members include Jeff Hagen, who strongly encouraged this line of inquiry; Lara Schmidt; Myron Hura; CAPT Scott Bunnay (U.S. Navy); Sarah A. Nowak; Akhil Shah; and Edward Wu. Donald Stevens, director of the Force Modernization and Employment Program within RAND Project AIR FORCE, also deserves special thanks. Second are our Air Force sponsors, Maj Gen Michael A. Keltz and Maj Gen Scott D. West, and action officers Lt Col Timothy O'Shea and Capt Jeff Crepeau. Third are the many individuals, notably reviewers, who looked at this document and shared their comments with the author: Forrest E. Morgan, Lt Gen (R) Robert J. Elder (U.S. Air Force), Mark Sparkman, Rena Rudavsky, Robert A. Guffey, and Jerry M. Sollinger. Finally, thanks go out to the National Academy of Sciences, which supported work on norms and narratives in cyberspace, material that Chapters Two and Three drew upon.

Abbreviations

C2	command and control
CNE	computer network exploitation
COCOM	combatant command
DDOS	distributed denial of service
DHS	U.S. Department of Homeland Security
DNS	Domain Name System
DPRK	Democratic People's Republic of Korea
FBI	Federal Bureau of Investigation
IP	Internet Protocol
ISP	Internet service provider
NATO	North Atlantic Treaty Organization
NTSB	National Transportation Safety Board
PAF	RAND Project AIR FORCE
PLA	People's Liberation Army
PSN	PlayStation Network
RF	radio frequency
SAM	surface-to-air missile

SecDef	Secretary of Defense
UAV	unmanned aerial vehicle
UN	United Nations
USCYBERCOM	U.S. Cyber Command
USSTRATCOM	U.S. Strategic Command

CHAPTER ONE

Introduction

The chances are growing that the United States will find itself in a cybercrisis—the escalation of tensions associated with a major cyberattack, suspicions that one has taken place, or fears that it might do so soon. By *crisis*, we mean an event or events that force a state to take action in a relatively short period or face the fraught consequences of inaction. Typically, because of fear that failure to act leads to war or a great loss of standing, states believe they must quickly decide whether to act.[1] When we use the term *cyberattack*, we refer to what may be a series of events that starts when systems are penetrated and may culminate in such events as blackouts, scrambled bank records, or interference with military operations.

The basis for such a forecast is twofold. First, the reported level of cyberincidents (most of which are crimes or acts of espionage) continues to rise. Second, risks arising from cyberspace are perceived as increasingly consequential; those perceptions are growing more quickly than the actual risks are.

A focus on international crises excludes attacks, however serious, carried out by individuals, criminals, or other nonstate actors, without serious help or after-the-fact protection from a foreign state. In the wake of nonstate attacks, the most-urgent priorities tend to be to restore services quickly and create conditions—which may include finding and punishing the perpetrators—that discourage further attacks. By this

---

[1] Richard Ned Lebow, *Between Peace and War: The Nature of International Crisis*, Baltimore, Md.: Johns Hopkins University Press, 1981, pp. 7–12, has a good discussion of the definition of *crisis*.

criterion, even a major cyberattack by al Qaeda would not be considered a cybercrisis for purposes of this report unless it were linked to a state. In the current environment, there would be, for instance, no serious prospect of hostile state action preventing either priority from being carried out.

Such a definition, with its implicit requirement for urgency, also largely excludes day-to-day activity in cyberspace. Although identity theft, intellectual property theft, and other forms of espionage may be large issues, they do not entail a challenge to national power and sovereignty that requires an immediate response in the international arena. That noted, the target state could choose to create a crisis over day-to-day events if it believes that foreign governments are aiding or shielding such hackers (much as the Austrians created an international crisis over the assassination by a Serbian national of an archduke in 1914, the event that led to the start of World War I), especially when the accumulation of effects crosses some threshold.

Some Hypothetical Crises

What might constitute a cybercrisis, or at least the beginning of one? In this section are seven examples for consideration. Each assumes clarity about the basics of what happened—at least at the level of understanding that something is not right in cyberspace—but there are still enough issues in dispute to raise tensions. What was the source of these faults that led to system malfunction? If intended, who carried them out? Under what command and control (C2) did they work? What was the intention of the perpetrators? Do these faults establish a new normal in cyberspace that can and ought to be accepted?

A list follows:

- Phony control signals in the electrical grid lead to extended mysterious periods of instability and intermittent loss of power. An examination of Supervisory Control and Data Acquisition code reveals malware that looks a lot like what has been conclusively but not publicly associated with a specific country. But what was the motive? Could the attack be a test of how the target could react, or a warning against something (but no one is sure of exactly what)?

- An extended period of interference with the Internet's Domain Name System (DNS) and routing algorithms lead to the extended denial of Internet service to an island that is the home to substantial military activities. The DNS and routing-algorithm attack seems quite suspicious, but even suspicious routing accidents may be exactly that.[2] If accidents are ruled out, then how such an outage is interpreted may depend on what happens in the relevant area: Is the attack a prelude to the use of military force? Unfortunately, how the victim reacts may make the matter moot. If one side believes that Internet outages will prevent its mobilizing assets for deployment, it may decide to premobilize these assets just in case. The alleged perpetrator—which may be completely innocent (a third party carried out the attack) or partially innocent (e.g., a rogue actor carried out the attack)—may observe only that assets are being mobilized and conclude that it, too, must countermobilize, also just in case.

- A simultaneous spate of intrusions has been detected against commercial enterprises. Although many of the first intrusions were detected and deleted by Internet service providers (ISPs), the technical sophistication of the intrusions have improved over the course of the evening to the point at which their signatures are fading and look likely to disappear entirely. The rapidly molting malware, clearly deliberate and clearly indicative of an advanced persistent threat, appears directed at organizations with a significant amount of intellectual property at risk. Do other countries fear that, if such malware, now impossible to detect, is allowed to work its way into such systems, its presence will effectively establish a new de facto norm on how much bad behavior will be considered tolerable?

---

[2] There have been considerable but unproven suspicions that a large diversion of Internet traffic to China that took place in 2010 may not have been an accident; see Elinor Mills, "Web Traffic Redirected to China in Mystery Mix-Up," *CNET*, March 25, 2010.

- A sophisticated attack against servers carrying traffic from a third country in turmoil has blocked all communications from that location that appear to carry images or video. This is followed by a malware attack on servers internal to that third country, which disables the servers' ability to filter out incoming messages based on politically sensitive keywords. Here, the issue may be less who did what and more who has the right to do what. Suspicion falls on those working for the country in turmoil, whose sympathizers retort that, except for a minor problem of exactly where the servers sat, the state had a right to manage outgoing and incoming traffic. Similarly, the attack on the firewall was perpetrated by hackers involved who may have been acting on their own but may have received support for more-legitimate activities from states. Important principles are at issue.
- A flash crash on major financial institutions leads to sharp reductions in the price of government-backed bonds just prior to a closely watched sale of a heavily indebted European country.[3] There seems to have been a wave of short-selling just before the crash. The European country had to withdraw the bond offering, forcing it to seek private financing, burdened with onerous provisions, with unnamed sovereign debt funds. Was the flash crash a result of panic, a hack, or a software glitch? If the latter, was it deliberate? If it was accidental, was it known about beforehand?
- Intermittent artifacts in weather reports (high winds, heavy rains) are interacting with guidance systems on medium-altitude unmanned aerial vehicles (UAVs) (operating just inside national borders) to send them away from certain sensitive terrain just beyond the borders. Without understanding the source of these artifacts, it is not clear how usable the UAVs would be in a crisis (ignoring the weather artifacts risks losing too many UAVs to bad weather; using scarcer high-altitude UAVs to chase ghosts may draw them away from higher-priority missions). Is some-

---

[3]   The Flash Crash was a U.S. stock market crash on May 6, 2010, in which the Dow Jones Industrial Average plunged about 1,000 points, or about 9 percent, only to recover those losses within minutes.

thing being planned in denied zones? If so, what mischief is being planned? Or are the artifacts being induced in order to see how the UAV operators react, also in preparation for mischief?

- A key power in cyberspace withdraws from United Nations (UN) negotiations on rules of the cyberroad and simultaneously announces the creation of a large fund to create a capacity for red-teaming attacks on critical infrastructures, for the purpose, it declares, of hardening its own systems. Several weeks earlier, it had published a vigorous strategy for cyberspace.[4] Does this action portend a shift toward more aggression in cyberspace? Are other countries being put on notice? Will their pro-Internet policies be characterized as naïve if they do not respond?

None of the incidents may spark a crisis. Alternatively, a crisis may start when a state decides that another state must alter its course or face consequences, or when it believes that current norms (e.g., tolerating cyberespionage because traditional espionage is tolerated) are responsible for some dramatic incident and they are therefore no longer acceptable.

Mutual Mistrust Is Likely to Characterize a Cybercrisis

Most crises take place between states that do not trust one another. Such states—not to mention their militaries and especially their intelligence agencies—are often mutually opaque as well. It is therefore easy for one to ascribe the worst motives to the other. Operations in cyberspace tend to be especially opaque, in large part because they tend to be handled by those parts of the national security establishment most inclined to keep secrets. Most states (Japan, perhaps excepted) are not shy about acknowledging their capacity for offensive kinetic combat, but, until mid-2012, few were willing to make the same state-

---

[4] Note that *deterrence* and *strategy* are both loaded words in Chinese. *Deterrence* connotes an active threat, while, in U.S. usage, the emphasis is on restraint, albeit imposed. *Strategy* is how to win a war, rather than, as in U.S. usage, how to structure means to achieve an end, which may not necessarily be military victory as such.

ment about their cybercapabilities.[5] Furthermore, although as Sun Tzu observed, all warfare is based on deception, cyberwarfare would be not just difficult but impossible without deception at the tactical end—which cannot help but bleed over into the operational and even strategic levels. Hence, the level of mistrust associated with incidents in cyberspace is likely to be particularly high.

Historically, worst-case thinking is conducive to crisis.[6] The descent into World War I, for instance, was characterized by each side's belief that its mobilization was defensive but those of its neighbors was offensive. Egyptian president Gamal Abdul Nasser's blockade of Sharm el Sheikh in 1967 was viewed in Israel as a preparation for war for which, in retrospect, Egypt had made no good preparation. GEN Douglas MacArthur's drive into North Korea was perceived by China as prefatory to an invasion (perhaps in conjunction with one from Taiwan).

Some of this worst-case thinking reflects perceptions about intent: "The other side would not have done this if it had not been hostile." Some of it, however, represents instrumental logic: "The other side did

---

[5] With some partial exceptions. In December 2011, the *Jerusalem Post* reported that Iran was planning to spend $1 billion on cyberdefenses and offenses (Yaakov Katz, "Iran Embarks on $1b. Cyber-Warfare Program," *Jerusalem Post*, December 18, 2011); this explicitly included offensive capabilities. In the same month, the defense authorization bill (Public Law 112-81, National Defense Authorization Act for Fiscal Year 2012, December 31, 2011) passed affirming that the U.S. Department of Defense may carry out offensive cyberattacks (J. Nicholas Hoover, "Defense Bill Approves Offensive Cyber Warfare," *InformationWeek*, January 5, 2012). According to Agence France-Presse reporting,

> Pre-emptive cyber strikes against perceived national security threats are a "civilized option" to neutralize potential attacks, Britain's armed forces minister said Sunday. Nick Harvey made the comment at the Shangri-La Dialogue security summit in Singapore in relation to reports that the US had launched cyber attacks to cripple Iran's nuclear program. . . . Britain's stance was supported by Canadian Defence Minister Peter Gordon MacKay, who likened a pre-emptive cyber strike to an "insurance policy", warning of the need to be prepared. ("Cyber Strikes a 'Civilized' Option: Britain," Agence France-Presse, June 3, 2012)

[6] It also supports treating low-probability events, if sufficiently catastrophic, as though they are likely enough to merit active suppression. See, for instance, Ron Suskind, *The One Percent Doctrine: Deep Inside America's Pursuit of Its Enemies Since 9/11*, New York: Simon and Schuster, 2007.

this because doing this was a step in the direction of further hostilities." Many actions evoke both reactions, and people cannot or do not always differentiate the two.

The logic that infers intent from a kinetic operation ought to echo the logic that infers intent from a cyberoperation because they both deal with the mind of the other side. But the mechanisms by which one kinetic operation sets up a conflict are likely to differ greatly from the mechanism by which a cyberoperation does so. Physics, military history, and verities of commanding military organizations together permit a fair guess as to what operations predispose others. None of the three applies to cyber, which has little physics, scant history, and few (if any) battle-tested rules for organizing forces. Thus, there are no well-grounded expectations of how to read a cyberattack as a precursor to military conflict.

Chinese theorists have postulated that a cyberattack on the logistics systems (and other systems, if an attacker can get at them) of U.S. forces could disrupt deployment across the Pacific and thereby tilt the balance of forces in China's direction. But no one is certain how long systems would be down, much less how great the damage would be or how badly crippled the U.S. military's operations would be as a result. The best guess is that the acute phase of the disruption would be measured in days (assuming that the logistics system is not taken offline to be cleaned) with chronic effects spread over weeks and months (depending on the capabilities of backup systems and the degree of corruption, if any, found within the databases themselves). But this is only a guess; it is hard to know what recovery times would be or, more to the point, what potential attackers *think* they might be (essentially, it requires assessing the performance of defenders that one has not met facing a situation they have not seen before). Thus, it is doubly unclear what might inform subsequent crisis management after a cyberattack has disabled military capabilities. The target state is likely to tune up the gain on its indication-and-warnings receivers if it believes that the disruption in its logistics systems portends imminent war—but turning up the gain increases the odds that the spurious signals will be read as precursors and then echoed back. We see this despite the possibility that outages in the logistics system could come from administrative error, software artifacts (notably, during updates), even deliberately induced errors from nonstate actors, third-party states hoping to profit from mischief, or, say, rogue operators in the hostile states. The logistics scenario, incidentally, has been well explored to the point at which it can be considered canonical. Interpreting noncanonical scenarios, such as when civilian capabilities in militarily sensitive locations have been disrupted, may give rise to wilder swings of imagination on the subject of how they may facilitate military operations, including even nuclear ones. After all, a great deal of nonsense on the military utility of cyberoperations has been published; even more-egregious nonsense may have been whispered.

The difficulties of understanding the implications of cyberoperations are compounded by the risk of miscalculating the purpose of computer network exploitation (CNE) (in contrast to taking unexpected exception to CNE as such) as intelligence preparation of the battlefield. True, states spy on the military systems of others. To the extent that CNE is like historical spying, the timing of success and disclosure may indicate nothing more than good and bad luck, respectively. Thus, disclosure should not normally suggest that the battlefield is being prepared for immediate use—unless the target reasons that the attackers' capture of temporary information about the state of the target system is important only for imminent combat. As it is, there is little indication that anyone confidently knows how to differentiate espionage from intelligence preparation of the battlefield at a technical level; indeed, it is unclear whether an implant that pries open a back door to a system can be distinguished from one primed to detonate on command (and thereby perhaps crash the system in which it is implanted). Bear in mind, from the crisis-management perspective, figuring out how to do this oneself solves only one part of the problem: If the target cannot do so, it may overreact if it finds out that its own systems are the battlefield that has been prepared by CNE.

Last is the problem of differentiating a cyberattack meant to damage something from one used to test the target's reaction. Tests in cyberspace are more plausible than tests in the physical world; the latter are visible (and, being visible, can create public pressure to respond), obvious, and can easily cause physical damage—perhaps even casualties. A cybertest and a kinetic test are both hostile, but the various ambiguities associated with cyberspace may persuade perpetrators that they can avoid the risk of getting caught.

Some crises are also punctuated by the confusion occasioned when standard operating procedures are deemed particularly aggressive or indicative. In cyberspace, standard operating procedures (except perhaps on defense) are less established, which is both better and worse for crisis management. One can imagine a state's leaders telling its cyberwarriors not to be provocative and its cyberwarriors retorting that this or that is part of standard operating procedures, only be to refuted by the claim that no standard operating procedure has yet become all that standard. This assumes, however, that the leaders are told what procedures their own forces carry out rather than being told (or worse, not told) by potential adversaries.

Can cybercrises be driven by popular sentiment? Sentiment-induced crises were common just over 100 years ago (e.g., Fashoda, the Spanish-American War, or the Agadir, Morocco, crisis of 1911). Although popular sentiment is somewhat more pacifist these days, notably in Europe, nationalism is still a potent force elsewhere. The Chinese government, for instance, found that it had to work hard to suppress nationalist sentiment in crises involving foreigners.[7] To date, there has been no mass popular reaction to cyber events.[8] Although the issue of Chinese hacking into U.S. corporations was independently raised by three candidates at the end of the November 2011 Republican foreign policy debate, it has generally not featured very prominently within the overall political season. Perhaps people (particularly in developing countries) expect computer systems to fail from time to time and may therefore not be overly excited if one of these failures

---

[7] In the late 1990s, a controversy between China and Japan over the ownership of the Diaoyu islands unleashed a wave of Chinese nationalism so intense that the Communist Party had to reverse its usual posture and actively suppress demonstrations. See Erica Strecker Downs and Phillip C. Saunders, "Legitimacy and the Limits of Nationalism: China and the Diaoyu Islands," *International Security*, Vol. 23, No. 3, Winter 1998–1999, pp. 114–146.

[8] Although people protested (even more vigorously) when Egyptian president Hosni Mubarak isolated Egypt from the Internet, the protests were against Mubarak and his attempt to silence protestors and not so much against their loss of service per se.

is produced by foreign hackers. Perhaps, therefore, popular sentiment would exacerbate matters only if leading politicians or pundits portrayed an incident as a challenge to a state's self-sufficiency or strength. A further guess is that, as hard as it is to teach leaders about the facts and issues involved in cyberattacks, teaching the public is harder still. Public reaction in a major cybercrisis may give new meaning to the concept of "wild card."

Overall, managing crises may be trickier if they involve cyberspace, *if they raise stakes that are comparable to those of crises that do not involve cyberspace.* The paucity of real cybercrises to date may reflect stakes that have yet to be very high. As for Stuxnet, in which a kinetic operation with the same effect (e.g., one-tenth as large as taking out Iraq's Osirak facility) would have raised tempers, many factors may have reduced the immediate effect. If nothing else, the time of the damage (probably late 2009, early 2010), the first indications among the technical community that an attack may have taken place (summer 2010), the point at which the attack was revealed to the public at large (early autumn 2010), and the point at which the target acknowledged having been attacked (late autumn 2010) were each spaced far from one another. In a kinetic operation, all four points would have fallen within the same 24-hour cycle. That attribution and damage assessment had large uncertainties as well also took some edge off the crisis.[9]

States May Have Room for Maneuver in a Cybercrisis

This monograph's normative treatment of cybercrises, at least from the U.S. perspective, is that crises are best avoided and, if unavoidable, then resolved quickly, with minimal losses. This is consistent with the United States being a peaceful status quo power. Its tendencies, if anything, should be stronger in cyberspace because U.S. dependence on

---

[9]   For an overall Stuxnet timeline, see Kim Zetter, "Stuxnet Timeline Shows Correlation Among Events," *Wired*, July 11, 2011. But see David E. Sanger, *Confront and Conceal: Obama's Secret Wars and Surprising Use of American Power*, New York: Crown Publishers, 2012, Chapter Eight, for a somewhat different timeline.

networked systems is as high as any other country's and higher than that of all of its strategic rivals.

Although such a posture argues against inventing or exacerbating crises (mostly[10]), it does not necessarily dictate downplaying real crises or pretending they do not exist. A great deal depends on whether other states are perceived as basically aggressive (and must be stopped) or defensive (and can be accommodated). During the Cuban missile crisis, many of President John F. Kennedy's advisers thought they saw another Munich:[11] A failure to respond forcefully would embolden the Soviet Union, discourage allies, and sow the seeds for a later confrontation when the United States would be in a worse position. President Kennedy, however, saw the potential for Sarajevo 1914; he carried Barbara Tuchman's *Guns of August* around with him, urging his advisers to read it.[12] His choice shows great concern with stumbling inadvertently into a nuclear war because one side's moves caused the other side to react in a hostile manner, forcing the first side to react accordingly, and so on.

In some circumstances, forgoing a vigorous response may create a new baseline for misbehavior in cyberspace. If the target state has advocated a standard for behavior and accepts the incident without too much protest, it signals a lack of seriousness in general, not just about cyberspace. The attacker and other states may read the failure to respond as evidence of weakness. If the incident has weakened the tar-

---

[10] Sometimes, even the United States may want a crisis. For instance, the United States can leverage a damaging cyberattack to justify going to war with a state that it needed to suppress (e.g., because it was building nuclear weapons). Without the cybercrisis, such a move would be regarded by some as naked aggression. With a crisis, some erstwhile doubters may be convinced that war would be justified. This works even better if the attacker can be maneuvered into a declaration of war (admittedly, an anachronism) or escalation that is tantamount to one. Otto von Bismarck, for instance, manipulated Napoleon III to declare war on Prussia in 1870 to complete his German unification project. See Michael Howard, *The Franco-Prussian War: The German Invasion of France, 1870–1871*, New York: Macmillan, 1962.

[11] The Munich Agreement, negotiated by major European powers other than Czechoslovakia, permitted Nazi Germany's annexation of Czechoslovakia's Sudetenland, areas along Czech borders that were inhabited primarily by ethnic Germans. It is widely regarded as a failed act of appeasement toward Germany.

[12] Barbara Wertheim Tuchman, *The Guns of August*, New York: Macmillan, 1962.

get's military, a failure to respond may portend military defeat. Finally, even if a state's leadership would rather let the incident pass, its ability to act (or not) may be constrained by domestic politics. Thus, even rational leadership acting with a cold eye may descend into crisis.

States can modulate their own actions to reduce the odds that another state has a legitimate or even quasi-legitimate motive to take things to crisis mode. Even Estonia in 2007—an innocent state doing no more than exercising its sovereign rights (to relocate a war monument)—had a choice about whether to make an international crisis of the wave of distributed denial-of-service (DDOS) attacks on government and commercial web sites.[13] True, it had a *domestic* crisis and needed to restore Internet services quickly. It also sought the North Atlantic Treaty Organization's (NATO's) support in declaring the attack a NATO Article V (common defense) matter. But, in the end, it wisely decided not to pick a fight with Russia. And, as a result of some engineering changes to its networks, Estonia is a harder target today.

Consider whether finding someone "planting logic bombs on the [electric] grid . . . would provoke the equivalent of the Cuban Missile Crisis"?[14] Should it? Analogies of this sort can be misleading. The United States forced a crisis over Cuba to persuade the Soviet Union to remove its missiles, something the United States could not do on its own without starting a war. Such pressure is not needed to remove implants that have already been found, and how could such an induced crisis be ended if no one can be sure whether implants that neither side has yet found have been deactivated? How wise is it to start a crisis when one cannot tell whether such a crisis has ended?[15] At what point

---

[13] The term *distributed* refers to the fact that almost all such attacks involve many subverted computers clogging the lines to the ultimate target. In fact, one sufficiently powerful computer can clog the lines to the ultimate target. Although this kind of single-computer attack is possible, it is also quite rare.

[14] As an unnamed military official argued as quoted in "Briefing: Cyberwar," *Economist*, July 3, 2010, p. 28.

[15] Presumably, the target would not tell the implanter about some of what was discovered and challenge the implanter to reveal the implants so that they may be deactivated. The implanter would then have to figure out what the target knew, to determine whether to

should states adopt 1-percent doctrines and analyze anomalies in terms of "worst-case" assumptions?

The evolution of a cybercrisis will reflect particularities of cyberspace.[16] Of note is likely the likelihood of confusion over who did what to whom. Such confusion may not dissipate quickly. The owners of a system may know that something went wrong. The attackers of a system may know what damage was intended. But neither will know what the other does, and the rest of the world may have little independent means of assessing anything. If and when a consensus forms on attribution, the character of a cybercrisis may undergo a profound change.

How quickly a state must respond to an incident is a matter of context and politics, not technology, as such. In the nuclear realm, there is a basis for thinking in terms of minutes (e.g., "launch on warning") because a large percentage of a state's offensive means could be lost in minutes. In cyberspace, in which effects are chancy and can often be reversed, the aim is to restore systems back to required service levels—something that can take place over hours or days. What matters afterward is not the speed of computers but the speed at which people can be influenced to stop attacking, largely because a state's ability to carry out cyberattacks is quite hard to disarm. News cycles are a better metric than computer cycles. Indeed, because cyberspace is such foreign terrain to national security decisionmakers (who then delegate strategic cyberattack decisions, because they do not grasp their ramifications[17]), additional time may be required to accommodate their efforts to grasp what is going on.

A cybercrisis will largely be what its participants say it is. Each side is likely to tell a different version, and neither side may have the facts required to prove as much. As with other crises but perhaps more

---

remove all of them or just claim as much, hoping that the ones left alone are those that the target had not and could not discover.

[16] Many of these were discussed in Martin C. Libicki, *Cyberdeterrence and Cyberwar*, Santa Monica, Calif.: RAND Corporation, MG-877-AF, 2009 (notably, Chapter Two).

[17] As was claimed by an Israeli journalist with regard to Israel's Prime Minister Benjamin Netanyahu.

so, each state's moves in a cybercrisis are likely to be shaped not only by strategic imperatives but also by what its participants wish to communicate about their values, fears, postures (e.g., "don't tread on me"), respect for norms, and their role in the international system. In other words, states may summon their own narratives to characterize events, explain their actions, and put the actions of others in a particular, generally negative, context.

In great contrast to physical war, in which a failure to respond means being overrun, the *direct security* implications of doing nothing in the face of a cyberattack may be small. Cyberattacks, even a series of them, may be less like physical warfare and more like raids (but with mostly temporary, nonkinetic effects), and states that do not respond to raids are not necessarily overrun as a result. Because retaliation cannot disarm the attacker, the failure to react has no bearing on the attacker's ability to do damage—only its willingness.[18]

Once a consensus emerges on at least who carried out the attack, the target state's room for maneuver may narrow. It may then feel itself challenged. The challenge may be direct if the attacker says so, justifying its act by citing, for instance, prior attacks (within or beyond cyberspace) or the need for preemption (of imminent attacks, whether cyber or kinetic). Or, the attacker may deny the attack directly but praise the attack (e.g., the attitude of Iran toward acts of Hezbollah). Or, the attacker may deny everything, but its spokespeople, official or otherwise, may emphasize the target's weakness in permitting an attack to succeed. The attacker could blandly deny everything (the Chinese flatly deny all cyberespionage accusations, for instance).

The target state, for its part, could characterize the attack as follows:

- a strategic error (e.g., the attacker thought, erroneously, it was hit first)

---

[18] The prerequisites for a cyberattack are few: Talented hackers, intelligence on the target, exploits to match the vulnerabilities found through such intelligence, a personal computer or any comparable computing device, and any network connection. See Libicki, 2009. Left implied in that report is that a cyberattack can affect only the computer or the network connection, both of which are ubiquitous and inexpensive and can be easily replaced.

- an inadvertence (e.g., the attack was an accidental or unsanctioned act carried out by a rogue faction or at the behest of the attacking government)
- a culmination (e.g., the act was undertaken to right a past wrong or as a warning shot to defuse an existing crisis, in either the real or virtual world)
- an operation to achieve a particular end, such as stalling a nuclear program
- a provocation undertaken as a signal or prefatory to more hostile action.

If the target fails to react, the attacker, itself, may not view forbearance negatively but as deserved in the first case (error), a blessing in the second case (inadvertence), and a statement of maturity in the third case (culmination). In the fourth case (instrumental), the failure to respond may put other targets at risk but only if the attacker has further operational goals. Only in the last case (provocation) might it view a failure to respond to be an act of weakness that merits further exploitation. But the target must also worry about what third parties think. In that case, would the attacker helpfully point out that the target's failure to respond harshly signifies not weakness but far-sightedness, or would the target so dislike attackers that it would neither accept nor acknowledge the latter's help with building its own narrative?

Clearly, understanding an attacker's motivation matters. How might it be sought? Forensics that indicate which state carried out the attack is only a start. Other clues come from knowing *who* in the state attacked and why. The target may elicit more clues by pressuring the attacker's state to condemn the attacker. Distinguishing between a culminating attack and a prefatory attack depends almost entirely on political evidence. Hints—but hardly proof—that the attack was culminating include statements to that effect, offers to reduce tensions, a visible turning to other matters, or a stand-down of forces (raising the question of how to detect when cyberforces stand down).

Throughout all this, states have a choice in how much to invest in reacting to incidents.

A Note on Methodology

The purpose of this monograph is to examine what is known or can be logically inferred about managing a cybercrisis through the lenses of existing theories of deterrence,[19] crisis management, and escalation management.

In the past 20 years, there have been plenty of instances of cybercrime and cyberespionage. But there have been only three and a half cyberattacks that could even conceivably rise to the level of a cyberwar: the DDOS attacks against Estonia in 2007, a similar attack on Georgia in 2008, the Stuxnet worm (2009–2010), and perhaps a cyberattack on Syria radar prefatory to an Israeli air strike on a supposed nuclear reactor in 2007.[20] Of these, all but one (Stuxnet) was unaccompanied by violence, which tends to create its own tensions. In part for this reason, none of these engendered a cybercrisis of the sort discussed here. As for generalizations about computer intrusion, they are based on reported cases; they exclude unreported proprietary or classified material.

As a result, the argument and conclusions in this report are not based on actual cybercrises but reflect reasoning about the potential causes and circumstances of cybercrises. This reasoning is based on the history of international relationships, extrapolations from the history of cybercrime and cyberespionage, and observations from how governments are approaching operating in cyberspace. It is also strongly colored by considerations of the art of the possible in cyberspace.

In years to come, the accumulation of evidence may permit a different perspective on these issues. Even without such evidence, what we know ten and 20 years hence may be different from what we know today because the nature of cyberspace, which, after all, is a human artifact, may have changed sufficiently. In the mid-1990s, the wily

---

[19] In Libicki, 2009, and again here, *deterrence* is used to mean deterrence by the threat of punishment. What others may call *deterrence by denial* is referred to by using such terms as *discouragement*.

[20] Opinion is mixed on whether Syrian radar was blinded by a cyberattack or by something more conventional, such as electronic warfare.

hacker[21] was the primary source of mischief in cyberspace. These days, the systematic effort to find vulnerabilities in systems and design to exploit code matter more.

The paucity of historical evidence, however, should not prevent making an educated guess about cyberwar and cybercrises, just as the lack of nuclear war hardly prevented earlier theorists from speculating on nuclear war and nuclear crises. Knowing as much, we can proceed.

Purpose and Organization

The genesis for this work was the broader issue of how the Air Force should integrate kinetic and nonkinetic—that is, cyber—operations.[22] Central to this process was careful consideration of how escalation options and risks should be treated, which, in turn, demanded a broader consideration across the entire crisis-management spectrum.

To put the material on escalation (Chapter Four) into a broader context, we preface the material with an examination of appropriate norms for international conduct with a focus on modulating day-to-day CNE and building international relationships (Chapter Two). Chapter Three addresses narratives, dialogue, and signals: what states can and should say about cybercrises. A state that would prevail has to make a clear story with good guys and bad guys without greatly distorting the facts (beyond their normal plasticity). Chapter Four assumes that a conflict has started and that the challenge is to keep it from becoming a strategic cyberwar or worse. If cyberwarfare is clearly subordinate to violent combat, then the control of the latter is likely to dominate the former. But, plausibly, cyberwar may take place in absence of violent combat, or the impact of cyberwar may be more salient: Its effects are global, while those of violent combat are local and far away. In the latter cases, the management of cyberconflict becomes central.

---

[21] From William R. Cheswick and Steven M. Bellovin, *Firewalls and Internet Security: Repelling the Wily Hacker*, Reading, Mass.: Addison-Wesley, 1994.

[22] There are other types of nonkinetic operations, such as psychological or information operations, but the study team treated nonkinetic as essentially cyber.

Thus, we examine and evaluate the range of actions the United States and other states can take both in advance of and during such crises. Implicit in the treatment is the notion that the best way to manage a crisis is to avoid having one start.

Chapter Five builds from that material to discusses strategic stability, largely to argue that crises are less likely to emanate from the unavoidable features of cyberspace and more likely to arise from each side's fear, often putatively exaggerated, of what may result from its failure to respond. Chapter Six asks and answers whether cyberdefenses can avoid cyberattacks.

This work also includes three appendixes, inserted to explain points that do not necessarily fit in the flow of the text. Appendix A discusses whether DDOS attacks matter as much as cyberattacks, and Appendix B describes the interaction of how attacks and responses depend on their overt nature and obviousness. Appendix C discusses whether good cyberdefenses can discourage cyberattacks.

CHAPTER TWO

Avoiding Crises by Creating Norms

Norms, we[1] now argue, can be an important component in modulating cybercrises, given some realism about what norms can or cannot do.

Those norms that call on states to separate themselves from freelance hackers and organized-crime elements not only make the ecosystem of cyberspace more trustworthy; they also limit the number and power of rogue actors that might otherwise go fishing in troubled waters. Those norms that require the victims of cyberattacks to exercise caution assigning responsibility to other states or in modulating how they respond can help spread oil on those troubled waters. Adroitly applying the laws of war to cyberspace represents another step in humanizing the barbarity of war, as paradoxical as it sounds.

Norms are no panacea, though. Enforcement is a problem in peacetime, although an agreement may be better than nothing. Wartime norms are even more difficult to enforce, partially because of the difficulty in distinguishing between their deliberate and accidental violation and partially because no cooperation can be expected from foes in clarifying or crediting reports of their violation. But, here too, the alternative is to do nothing.

At the very least, there is growing interest in the topic. In mid-2010, a 15-member negotiating committee working under UN authority generated a set of motherhood-and-apple-pie norms to govern the

---

[1] And the U.S. government, if the *International Strategy for Cyberspace* (Barack Obama, *International Strategy for Cyberspace: Prosperity, Security, and Openness in a Networked World*, Washington, D.C.: White House, May 2011) is indicative.

behavior of member nations.[2] By that point, bilateral negotiations had begun with Russia over behavior in cyberspace, and similar explorations have already begun with China.[3] Someone must believe that all this activity may result in something.

What Kind of Norms Might Be Useful?

Norms may be helpful in averting crises arising from misperception, mistakes, or misattribution. Taking up affirmative obligations to assist builds trust. Those that persuade states to dissociate themselves from nonstate hackers (lest evidence of linkages be found and publicized) make it easier for states so accused to deny complicity and thus harder for targets of cyberattack to make credible accusations of complicity. Abjuring espionage that would precede attacks on infrastructure may lower the tension level among states by reducing the expectations of strategic conflict in cyberspace.

Norms may help modulate crises as well. As mutual suspicion rises, every suspicious incident in cyberspace is likely to be interpreted as an underhanded maneuver by one or another side under cover of a third party, so assigned to preserve deniability. If such states have a record of staying away from rogue hackers, their denials may be more likely to be believed.

Enforce Laws Against Hacking

In 2000, the author of the "I Love You" virus escaped prosecution because his activities were not illegal in the Philippines. This oversight was corrected within a year.[4] Most of the states of concern to the United

---

[2]   John Markoff, "Step Taken to End Impasse Over Cybersecurity Talks," *New York Times*, July 16, 2010.

[3]   Brian Grow and Mark Hosenball, "Special Report: In Cyberspy vs. Cyberspy, China Has the Edge," Reuters, April 14, 2011.

[4]   Carlo Ito, "A Brief History of Nefarious Internet Hacking in the Philippines," *SourcingTrust*, March 30, 2011.

States have outlawed hacking. Nevertheless, the norm that cybercrime is illegal ought to be noted, if only for the sake of completeness.

Yet, many states have proven reluctant to cooperate in further investigations, much less extraditions, particularly if the hackers appear to be working on behalf of state interests. Fighting cybercrime is difficult and expensive. Many states are unwilling to pay the cost, particularly when it is others that would benefit.[5] Many such hackers are considered heroes at home. Thus, such a norm would be a real change. States would have to agree to help find hackers, particularly those who have victimized citizens of other states. This can be called an *obligation to assist*.

Exactly how to ensure enforcement is a tricky question. Although tolerating hackers can be bad for their business environment, even NATO's newest members, the countries of eastern Europe, have a hard time keeping the lid on organized cybercriminals.[6] There is little indication that states will agree to bend their sovereignty—and the notion that such states would not or could not carry out such investigations themselves is an insult (howsoever merited). How likely is it that they will make an exception for cybercrime when they do not for other crimes?[7] That said, even Russia and China have, themselves, prosecuted hackers when ignoring them was not in the state's interest.[8]

---

[5] Some argue that such countries as Russia or China could find hackers if they wanted to because they monitor their citizens intensively enough to catch hackers who would not be caught in the West, with its civil liberties. But would Western states be comfortable demanding that such countries find hackers by using methods that their own investigators would not be allowed to use?

[6] See, for instance, Yudhijit Bhattacharjee, "Why Does a Remote Town in Romania Have So Many Cyber-Criminals?" *Wired*, February 2011, pp. 82–87, 124.

[7] Federal Bureau of Investigation (FBI), "FBI, Slovenian and Spanish Police Arrest Mariposa Botnet Creator, Operators," Washington, D.C., July 28, 2010.

[8] John Leyden, "Russian Bookmaker Hackers Jailed for Eight Years," *Register/Enterprise Security*, October 4, 2006 (this example may be a singular action, however, because it alone appears in multiple citations); Keith Bradsher, "China Announces Arrests in Hacking Crackdown," *New York Times*, February 8, 2010a. Investigators themselves may technically have to commit crimes to trace bad packets through routers that will not disgorge their contents freely. The Snooping Dragon investigation, no doubt, had to (Shishir Nagaraja and Ross Anderson, *The Snooping Dragon: Social-Malware Surveillance of the Tibetan Movement*, Cam-

The associated notion that states have to be responsible for the bad packets that leave their borders is less helpful. Even if a state satisfies an obligation to assist foreign law enforcement or mount its own enforcement, there is no guarantee that all that effort would mean that all hackers get caught. Responsibility assumed is no substitute for attribution.

This suggests another norm: If an attack on a system is deemed off-limits even during wartime, then espionage to collect intelligence prefatory to an attack on such a system should be off-limits. Collecting information is a weak excuse for penetrating a system if owners of society's more sensitive systems (e.g., for hospitals, electric power production) are willing to share technical information without fear of losing business to overseas vendors. Thus, if a state learns, against all odds, of such an implant from another state put into a sensitive system, the burden of proof that such an implant was for espionage rather than sabotage should rest on the accused, not the accuser. All this presumes that states believe that cyberattacks on national infrastructures should also be forsworn.[9] This raises a dilemma: Do states that forswear cyberattacks on infrastructures thereby put themselves in a position in which they have to forswear physical attacks on national infrastructures? If so, is the United States—which, in 1999, attacked Serbian bridges and commercial facilities belonging to friends of Slobodan Milošević and, in 1991 and 2003, attacked power plants in Iraq—ready to do this?

Dissociate from Freelance Hackers

Another norm would have states dissociate themselves from criminal or freelance hackers. The practice is strategically deceptive because it permits states to get the benefit of criminal activity without necessarily having to face the international condemnation of whatever such hack-

---

bridge, UK: University of Cambridge, Computer Laboratory, Technical Report 746, March 2009).

[9] "Retired General Michael Hayden . . . also said ideas have been raised about forming the cyber equivalent of demilitarized zones for sensitive networks, such as the power grid and financial networks, that would be off-limits to attack from nation states" (Kim Zetter, "Former NSA Director: Countries Spewing Cyberattacks Should Be Held Responsible," *Wired*, July 29, 2010).

ers do. Such association also closely echoes the association between certain governments (notably, Iran) and terrorist groups (notably, Hamas and Hezbollah). Such an association is also bad policy. States can corrupt themselves by so doing, may overlook nonhacking crimes carried out by its favored hackers, and may be subject to blackmail: A criminal group under pressure for nonhacker activities could threaten to reveal its links to state-sponsored crimes in cyberspace. An important advantage of distinguishing government spying on the one hand and government-sponsored or -abetted spying by criminals or rogue elements on the other is that those performing the latter may have their own reasons to carry out cyberespionage; if they have a criminal interest in spying on systems that support critical infrastructure, their activity may be indistinguishable from preparations for a state-sponsored cyberattack. Worse, freelance activities of those who used to or appear to be operating on the state's behalf may entangle states in unwanted crises. If a state made a good-faith effort to act against those operating on its behalf, whether for commercial or "patriotic" reasons, victims of such cyberattacks may be more inclined to believe the state when it professes innocence.

Discourage Commercial Espionage

A similar norm might distinguish between time-honored national security espionage and all other espionage. Indeed, spying in the interests of national security may even contribute to international stability: Fears of a nuclear missile contest were assuaged by reports from U.S. spy satellites circa 1960. By contrast, commercial espionage is simply theft of intellectual property or identifying information, or worse (if taking personal information creates the opportunity for blackmail of individuals).

Strictures against commercial espionage may be more effectively enforced in the commercial realm of trade laws and trade courts than in the strategic realm of threat and counterthreat. If one could establish that corporations get an unfair advantage in foreign trade from having stolen information, might countries whose corporations were victimized bar entry to such products much as they might bar products that violate patents? What level of proof would be required before nations unilaterally declare it so—particularly before trade courts that are much less comfortable deciding facts than they are deciding law? As another sanction, winking at the theft of intellectual property ought to affect a state's good standing within the international trade community. That noted, will states that think they need CNE for economic development comply or be party to negotiations that could deprive them of such capabilities?

Be Careful About the Obligation to Suppress Cybertraffic

Roughly one-sixth of all the DDOS traffic directed against Estonia in 2007 came from computers that sit within the United States.[10] Should and can the U.S. government be required to take action to stem the flood? Should its ISPs accept the responsibility to block such packets, and should their governments indemnify them against angry customers if they do so? Is it even possible to stop errant packets to an address under attack without stopping all packets? Should ISPs proactively identify customers whose computers have become bots (that is, under the control of a hacker) and deny them access to the Internet until they clean themselves up?

Maybe not. Such obligations may not constitute cost-effective *domestic* practice even if the Internet were solely a U.S. phenomenon. Thus, calling for them *internationally* may make no more sense. Finally, as argued in Appendix A, the notion of a serious cybercrisis created by a flooding attack is remote.

How Do We Enforce Norms?

Enforcement is a tough problem. Although it is obvious when foreign or international law enforcement officials are barred from looking for evidence sitting in another state, otherwise proving that a state is not cooperative is difficult. Who can say that a state is failing to put in the requisite resources? Proving that a government pals with hackers, car-

---

[10] Robert Giesler, remarks, Center for Strategic and International Studies Global Security Forum 2011, June 8, 2011.

ries out cyberespionage, places implants in critical infrastructures, or spies on sensitive sites that have no national security value is akin to the difficult problems of attribution.

The argument for unenforceable norms reflects the tenet that hypocrisy is the price that vice pays to virtue. If states continue to declare certain actions in cyberspace to be illegitimate, then they have established a standard to which others can hold them. To the extent that such norms are recognized by national bureaucracies, such as those of Western countries, which take official guidance seriously, leaders must explain continually to their minions that the contrary is true if they wish to continue their cybermischief. Granted, in certain countries, brazen denial of the obvious is standing practice, but most countries wish to assume a somewhat consistent narrative for themselves and so, it is argued, will eventually slouch in the direction in which their words take them. The history of the 1976 Helsinki Accords gives hope that norms may actually do something. Even though the Soviet Union and its Warsaw Pact allies had little intention of implementing its human rights accords, dissident groups in those countries, such as Moscow Helsinki Group and Charter 77, insisted that they do so—an insistence that further reduced the legitimacy of communist rule.

Norms may also have a demonstration effect. A group of respected states signs up to such norms. Other states may be convinced that associating with such an esteemed group requires that they, too, follow or at least pay lip service to such norms. Many Latin American countries have yielded, for instance, to the European Union's insistence that norms on the protection of personal information be built into their laws. The more that states follow norms, the greater the pressure on laggard states to conform. If *association* means peer status within the world's communication networks,[11] then the pull of example may be strong. Conversely, the ambiguities of cyberspace—who is investing in what, who has done what to whom—pose serious challenges to the

---

[11] Within the limits set by membership within the International Telecommunication Union (a UN-chartered institution) which makes certain communication rights of states inalienable regardless of their behavior in cyberspace.

demonstration model. Raising the stakes may also encourage other states or nonstate actors to take greater pains to expose such bad behavior on the part of others: They could establish monitoring mechanisms, recruit whistleblowers, or even set up sting operations. If the citizens of the potential rogue state take issue with a state's breaking its promises, they are less likely to cooperate and more likely to tell.

Norms also create a standard by which other states can judge cheaters. A state may not be able to prove anything—but it can compare its estimate of another state's behavior with the state's promises to rate the state's trustworthiness. A corporation, for instance, does not need proof before it decides to avoid investing in certain countries; a lack of trust suffices. True, mistrust often begets mistrust. But as long as being in good stead with advanced states has value, then those on the outside have to avoid being mistrusted by those on the inside more than the reverse. Good behavior may count even more if momentum builds behind cloud computing—outsourcing system functions to servers located in those countries that offer the best package of price, performance, and protection. Would such business gravitate to servers in countries that customers do not trust to respect their intellectual property? One might imagine that a Chinese firm may avoid putting its data in nations, such as Germany, that have complained about Chinese behavior in cyberspace, but the cloud that holds its data may not care about the politics.

Confidence-Building Measures

Confidence-building measures provide another tool to forestall the emergence of crises among mutually suspicious but not necessarily antagonistic states.

One such measure would be to cooperate in the investigation of specific incidents (almost all of which these days are acts of cyberespionage or cybercrime rather than cyberwar). Systems in one country are often penetrated by what appears to be hackers from another. Granted, some are opportunistic hop-throughs (e.g., the Russians get to U.S. targets by routing through Chinese servers). Yet, it may not be clear that all of them are. Investigation would help clear up suspicions on either side, if they are groundless. True, sovereign states may restrict the techniques that may be used to investigate crimes: Search warrants, for instance, are required for many forms of investigation in the United States. But, perhaps two states may reassure one another by each nominating an incident whose trail appears to lead to the other country and establish a one-time fact-finding "tiger team" as a way of prototyping investigative techniques that can form a model for future cooperation in clarifying cyberincidents.

Another method would be to establish bilateral or multilateral institutions to carry out important tasks. One might be to search for vulnerabilities in commonly used software.[12] Such a team would scrutinize such products looking for undocumented vulnerabilities that would then be reported to these companies as a spur to get these vulnerabilities closed. By creating such a team, membership in which may be drawn from participating states, not only would technical cooperation be gained on a problem that spans international borders—there may also be progress in developing useful analytical techniques that may be shared to improve the worldwide production and oversight of software and software-related products.

A related measure would be to establish a persistent round table coupled with research support to harmonize what other states understand to be the use of force in cyberspace. The risk is that, in a cybercrisis, one or another country might carry out acts that may be interpreted much more severely on one side than on the other. With such misinterpretation, the risk exists that both sides carry out increasingly hostile acts, each convinced that it is responding to escalation from the other side but that it is not itself escalating. Agreement over what constitutes not only the use of force but also other red lines in cyberspace would allow both sides to manage potential crises in cyberspace using a

---

[12] Although there is considerable work being carried out by academic institutions, freelancers, and some cyberdefense organizations in bug-hunting, this is an area in which further resources and organizational backing would not hurt.

common terminology.[13] This is one path for reducing potential friction over future crises in cyberspace.

The trick for confidence-building measures—as with signals (see Chapter Three)—is that those who would reassure have to take some risk of loss or exposure if they are insincere. Consider a state that grants investigators scope to investigate cybercrimes in its own country. If each state gets to choose the crimes that investigators can investigate, it can easily select those that it believes will indict those about which it cares little; only by allowing the *other state* to choose the activities that it can investigate will it risk being embarrassed if the hackers have ties or are otherwise condoned by their state. Similarly, the antivulnerability team risks finding vulnerabilities that one side has already found but has kept hidden hoping to use it in some future cyberattack. Although discussions on comparable red lines offer little comparable risk, it may put bounds on future narrative behavior ("we regard what you think is a small incident as a major one").

Norms for Victims of Cyberattacks

Purported victims of cyberattack may also mitigate crises if they, too, follow certain norms. States may obligate themselves not to jump to conclusions. Accusations have to be reasonable and coupled with mutual transparency: the plaintiffs in forming conclusions, and the defendants in assisting investigations. Such norms are not exclusive to cyberspace. Similar issues apply to disputes in outer space or over terrorism, organized crime, and military exercises. Cyberspace, however, is subject to great ambiguity—and, although the manipulation of ambiguity may be part of cyberstrategy, the elimination of ambiguity helps prevent inadvertent cybercrises.

---

[13] For a more detailed discussion, see Forrest E. Morgan, Karl P. Mueller, Evan S. Medeiros, Kevin L. Pollpeter, and Roger Cliff, *Dangerous Thresholds: Managing Escalation in the 21st Century*, Santa Monica, Calif.: RAND Corporation, MG-614-AF, 2008. Morgan et al., 2008, pp. 23–28, explains the mechanism of inadvertent escalation. Later (pp. 163–165), it discusses clarifying thresholds as a means of managing the risks of inadvertent escalation.

Norms may also help states distinguish between acts that merit diplomatic and judicial responses and those that could demand a forceful response. States violate such norms by reacting to lesser infractions as if to greater ones. Adherence would lend predictability to crises by modulating the action-reaction cycle. In pithier terms, such a norm would answer the questions what constitutes an act of war in cyberspace, and what are legitimate casus belli?[14] An international consensus that CNE is *not* a legitimate casus belli would be a start. It may also address whether thresholds or some other criteria might distinguish small cyberattacks appropriate for diplomatic or judicial responses from large ones that constitute casus belli. If there is a consensus there, what are these thresholds, and how are they to be measured? Furthermore, is it less fair to impose the same metrics on all target states (especially if measured, say, in dollars in a world in which gross domestic product varies greatly among states)? If not, how much variation is reasonable?[15]

Norms for War

Norms that apply the laws of armed conflict to cyberspace are armed with good intentions, but, by the time such laws can be tested or enforced, states have left the crisis mode and entered the war mode. As such, war norms have little direct bearing on crisis management.

Nevertheless, the development of norms—coupled with the confidence that they are being respected—may have an indirect stabilizing effect. If each state's society were accorded sanctuary status, each state would be able to regard the prospect of cyberwar more calmly. Perhaps. But do the *technical* characteristics of cyberwar permit a clean crosswalk between the laws of armed conflict as they apply in physical space

---

[14] See, for instance, Charles J. Dunlap, Jr., "Perspectives for Cyber Strategists on Law for Cyberwar," *Strategic Studies Quarterly*, Spring 2011, pp. 81–99, or Matthew Waxman, "Cyber-Attacks and the Use of Force: Back to the Future of Article 2(4)," *Yale Journal of International Law*, Vol. 36, No. 2, 2011, pp. 421–459.

[15] The United States, having survived Hurricane Katrina, could probably weather a cyberattack that cost it $100 billion in damage and lost work time, but how many other countries could do so?

and laws and their application in cyberspace? Consider, therefore, the treatment of deception, military necessity, proportionality, neutrality, and reversibility (a norm generally inapplicable in kinetic warfare but possible with electronic warfare and some space operations).

Deception

The laws of armed conflict outlaw many forms of deception.[16] Notably, they forbid perfidy, such as deception that would draw fire onto non-combatant targets, harming innocent people. False-flagging, disguising combatants as noncombatants, and disguising combat facilities as or locating them in legally protected structures, such as churches or hospitals, are similarly forbidden. This, in part, explains why lawful combatants are those that wear uniforms.

But deception is the sine qua non of cyberwar. If a message sent to a target system announced "hey, I'm a cyberattack," the target system would filter it out—this, for instance, is precisely the purpose of malware protection. Cyberoffenders, in turn, take comparable pains to elude these detection mechanisms by masquerading as legitimate traffic.

Another form of deception entails making an unimportant system or network look interesting in order to persuade attackers to waste their time rummaging through it, show their cybertechniques to the defender, and leave the system satisfied with their fool's gold. Honeypots or honeynets[17] are well-understood and legitimate defense tactics.

Should norms proscribe making military systems look like civilian systems in order to persuade offenders to roam elsewhere? The ability to

---

[16] Yet, not all forms of deception in war are prohibited by the laws of armed conflict. Military forces often make extensive use of mock-ups and decoys to draw errant fire and even use false communications to suggest they are in, or heading for, a location different from their true intention. In World War II, for instance, the Anglo-American allies conducted an extensive deception campaign, which included all of the above and more, to convince the Germans that the D-Day invasion would occur at Pas-de-Calais rather than Normandy. All of it was legal.

[17] A honeypot is a system that is established and engineered to attract hackers and then monitor how they attacked the system. A honeynet is a network of honeypots.

hide looks different in the physical and the cyberworlds. In the physical world, walls and roofs can mask what goes on inside a building—thus, indications on the outside can belie what goes on inside. In cyberspace, visibility can go all the way through or at least penetrate here and there. Conversely, in the real world, if walls and floors were invisible, it would be extraordinarily difficult to make the activities of a military C2 center look like the activities of a hospital. It may be difficult to tell what a given organization does simply by looking at, say, systems that manage its network. Thus, although some aspects of a civilian infrastructure may be easy to distinguish from a military infrastructure when seen from cyberspace, other aspects may be harder. These latter may include general system maintenance functions, which, if disrupted, can cripple the functions they support.

Military Necessity and Collateral Damage

Can one avoid cyberattacks on civilian targets when seeking to strike the military? Often—especially when military networks are air-gapped (that is, electronically separate from publicly accessible networks), as prudent military network management may suggest—but not always, particularly if the target seeks to immunize itself by daring the attacker to create collateral damage.

Attackers may have no way to know what service dependencies are. Some of this applies in the physical world. An attack on a power plant that cuts power to a military facility could also cut power to a civilian facility, but the visible artifacts of power distribution afford a guess as to what is connected to what. In cyberspace, neither physics nor economics yields particularly good clues as to which servers satisfy which clients (although hacking into the server may reveal this information). With cloud computing, a single server farm may support very different customers, many perhaps in neutral or even friendly countries.[18] The problem is not just one of linking a service to its owner. A bottleneck can result from disrupting an obscure but widely used ser-

---

[18] In June 2011, the FBI "seized Web-hosting servers from a data facility . . . , causing a number of sites to go down or transfer operations to other facilities." See Steven Musil, "FBI Seizes Web Hosting Company's Servers," *CNET*, June 21, 2011.

vice, e.g., one that reconciles different names found in databases into the same identity.

Avoiding gratuitous harm is a legitimate goal for cyberwar as with physical war, but, in either case, doing so depends on some cooperation from the victim. Thus, if the cyberattacker discovers that a particular system exists exclusively for civilian purposes, its disruption or corruption cannot be justified by military necessity. This goes double for attacks on systems that affect civilian health and safety. Thus an attack on a dam's control systems that causes it to release too much water and therefore floods a city below it would be considered illegitimate; the same applies to attacking medical files that indicate which medicines go to which people. The target state, correspondingly, has an obligation not to commingle systems so that an attack on a legitimate target does not damage protected targets, or at least not commingle them more than business logic would otherwise dictate.

So, how much should attackers have to know of target systems to discharge their responsibility to conform to the laws of armed conflict? If the knowledge were deficient and damage resulted, would opacity on the part of the adversary mitigate the attacker's responsibility? What constitutes a reasonable presumption of connectedness? What constitutes an unreasonable refusal by the attacker to exercise due diligence in examining such connections? Does sufficient sophistication to carry out a certain level of cyberattack presuppose sufficient sophistication to determine collateral damage?

The use of worms and viruses presents a tricky case. They appear indiscriminate and hence contrary to the laws of war, but, as Stuxnet proved, they are useful in getting into closed systems.[19] Would it be making too fine a point to differentiate between the understandable use of replicating malware as a delivery vehicle and the condemnable use of such malware as an instrument of indiscriminate disrup-

---

[19] Stuxnet propagated lustily enough to infect more than 100,000 machines. But Stuxnet was designed as a worm precisely to maximize the number of computers at the target site that would be infected, the better to raise the odds that someone would transfer a USB drive from an infected computer to a computer within the "air-gapped" centrifuge complex where the target industrial programmable logic controllers sat. Organizations that did not have the sought-for programmable logic controllers on their networks would not be damaged.

tion (particularly because many third parties had to expend time and money to clean Stuxnet out of their systems)?

Proportionality

Proportionality is tricky in all domains. If A hits B and B has grounds to believe that hitting back as hard would not deter subsequent attacks by A, B may conclude that it must hit back much harder to convince A to cease. In cyberspace, the problem of attribution strengthens the logic favoring overmatch: If an attacker can expect to carry out *most* cyberattacks with impunity, then the few times attribution is good enough for retaliation may justify striking back hard enough to make the statistical *expectation of retaliation* an effective deterrent.[20] That noted, proportionality is a norm not only because it is just but also because it is prudent if the attacker can counterretaliate. A disproportionate tit for tat is easily escalatory.

Even if the *principle* of proportionality does not apply to cyberspace the same way it does in physical space, practical problems exist in modulating effects in cyberspace to preserve proportionality. Physical attacks at least have the "advantage" of physics and chemistry with which to work in predicting the damage they will do. Because the blast radius of a 1,000-pound bomb is fairly well understood, one can know what definitely lies outside the blast radius and what definitely

---

[20] Compare this with LTG Keith Alexander's testimony (Keith Alexander, "Advance Questions for Lieutenant General Keith Alexander, USA, Nominee for Commander, United States Cyber Command," statement to the U.S. Senate Committee on Armed Services, April 15, 2010, p. 21):

> Criminal law models depend on deterrence as well. Legal scholars have argued that crimes that often go unsolved (vandalism, for example) should be punished more harshly to ensure an effective example is offered in the few cases where it's available. Under this model, the US should take swift and effective action in every case in which it can attribute an offensive action to a particular adversary.

Three pages later, however, he said,

> A commander's right to general self-defense is clearly established in both US and international law. Although this right has not been specifically established by legal precedent to apply to attacks in cyberspace, it is reasonable to assume that returning fire in cyberspace, as long as it complied with law of war principles (e.g., proportionality) would be lawful.

lies inside. In cyberspace, battle damage may depend on details of the target system that the attacker does not know. Error bands in cyberspace are therefore probably much wider, and they are measured in virtual rather than physical terms.[21] Broadly put, the likelihood that an attack designed to ensure that some minimum effect creates disproportionately harsh effects may well be higher in cyberspace than in physical space.

The risk that an attack may harm the unintended (collateral damage) or overly harm the intended (disproportionate damage) suggests some norms for constructing exploits. Stuxnet provides a good example largely because, as a worm, it spread on its own from one computer to another. Even though its payload was very tightly specified (it was only meant to harm a very specific type of Siemens controller), it infected nearly 100,000 computers, a large share of which were in Iran. This required a great deal of cleanup.[22] Because the worm was not programmed to turn itself off until 2012, it lingered long enough to be discovered. Had Stuxnet been written to turn itself off if it found itself outside Iran's Internet protocol (IP) address space, or if its time to live were not so long, such problems might have been avoided (albeit, perhaps, at a somewhat lower likelihood of mission success). The more likely risk, however, is not that the exploit will go out of control (advanced-persistent-threat attacks, for instance, do not spread by means of worms) but that the fault induced by the exploit may have unexpected ramifications. There might be ways of designing exploits that step gingerly forward, testing to make sure that the expected damage is within bounds, but, until such designs are validated, expecting attackers to adhere to such designs would be premature.

The victim's responsibility for the damage done, conversely, may be a bigger issue in cyberspace than in physical space. Iraq launched

---

[21] Although it may take detailed knowledge of the other side's systems to understand what is close or far away in virtual terms, some effects can be tailored more precisely: One can corrupt files A and C without worrying about an intermediate file B.

[22] The Russian ambassador to NATO called for an investigation into Stuxnet on the grounds that it could have launched a new Chernobyl (as quoted by Agence France-Presse in "Russia Calls for NATO Probe into Iran Cyber Strike," Agence France-Presse, January 26, 2011). Such a claim appears far-fetched, though.

Scud missiles against both Iran in the 1980s and Israel in 1991. Far fewer people died per missile launch in Israel,[23] partly because its construction standards are better than those in Iran. Notwithstanding whether *any* such terror weapons can be justified, can Iraq be held responsible for the high level of casualties in Iran, whose construction standards should not have come as a surprise? Matters are more opaque in cyberspace. In theory, well-written software should not be made to operate in ways that breaks hardware, but flawed software and promiscuous connections among systems that allow faults in one to infect the other exist. An act of retaliation meant to disrupt electricity for just a few days may cause power-generating hardware to fail unexpectedly, disrupting electricity for months. Would such damage lead others to judge such retaliation to be disproportionate? If a system administrator is practicing security through obscurity and therefore makes it difficult for attackers to know whether disrupting or corrupting an operation has serious downstream attacks, does this create at least some responsibility when an attack meant to have specific effects instead has general ones?

Reversibility

One potential norm appropriate for cyberspace (with little counterpart in the physical world) is reversibility: Every attack that takes place would have an antidote, and the antidote should be made available to the target when hostilities cease.[24] Thus, an attack that encrypts the only copy of someone's data should be followed by transfer of a decryption key when peace breaks out. Similarly, an attack that corrupts data should be followed by transfer of the true data.

Reversibility has practical difficulties. Sometimes, it is not necessary. CNE requires no antidote because nothing is broken. Most

---

[23] Roughly 200 missiles killed 2,000 people in Iran, but, against Israel, 42 missiles killed only one Israeli directly. That noted, Tehran is far closer to Iran than Tel Aviv is, thus allowing more Scuds to reach closer to their intended target.

[24] A similar norm may be for each side to remove its implants from the systems of the other. The latter norm brings up two issues: enforcement (how would one side know that what implants the other side has not removed) and the recognized legitimacy of espionage (not all implants are used for attack).

attacks meant for disruption or even corruption can be reversed by the target's system administrators well before peace breaks out. In many cases, the corrupted or encrypted data (e.g., the status of spare parts inventories) has a short half-life; by war's end, restoration would be meaningless. However, this tenet imposes a requirement to refrain from attacks unless there *is* an antidote—much as those who lay mines should remember where they put them. Thus, a corruption attack would not be allowed to randomize data unless the true records were stored somewhere else. Sometimes, such storage is infeasible: Storing the precorrupted data locally or sending them offsite may cue defenders that something strange is going on, and there may be no opportunity to ship the data back anyway.

Conclusions

International agreements can help reduce the odds of a cybercrisis, but only if their limited role is understood. Norms to govern state behavior in peacetime may be useful even if they cannot be enforced. They put states on record against certain behaviors. Even if these states sign in bad faith, others—perhaps their own citizens or someone who balks when asked to overlook the violation of such norms—will be there to remind them whenever something takes place out of bounds. Norms help tamp down crises by separating states from certain forms of malfeasance and, by so doing, may add a few rays of clarity to otherwise ambiguous and suspicious activities. Norms that govern the use of cyberattacks in wartime may also be useful, but, with enforcement so difficult, enthusiasm about their beneficial effect should be tempered.

Because, as a general rule, states that trust each other rarely go to war against one another, the more useful norms are those that can be monitored before any war starts. Thus, those that pledge nations to cooperate in investigate cybercrimes, that sever bonds between a state and its commercially oriented cybercriminals, and that frown deeply on espionage on networks that support critical public services (e.g., electrical power) can be useful. The United States can sign without reservations, and the signatures of others can be useful checks on their actions.[25] Conversely, norms that are inherently hard to monitor and reward cheating (e.g., against cyberweapons) or that bias cyberspace against states that believe in legislating national security behavior are far less desirable. Norms that can be enforced only in wartime are probably unlikely to be helpful when most needed because monitoring and enforcement are nearly impossible at the time.

Working toward useful norms may well help reduce the likelihood of a crisis, but it would be unrealistic to believe that they can, even in concert, eliminate the possibility. The next two chapters discuss how states can and could manage such crises.

---

[25] Much depends on what other norms other states would require before they sign up. Norms that reinforce a state's ability to censor the Internet within its own boundaries, for instance, would not be well received in the United States.

CHAPTER THREE

Narratives, Dialogue, and Signals

The writer Tom Wolfe used to argue that modern art had "become completely literary: the paintings and other works exist only to illustrate the text."[1] Using this insight, he argued that a modern art museum that, like classical art museums, had large paintings and small explanations of them should instead have large explanations with small paintings in order to illustrate the point. So, too, with narratives about cyberwar. What happened may pale compared with what people say happened. Perhaps more than any other form of combat, cyberwar is storytelling—not inappropriately for a form of conflict that means to alter information.

Thus, offensive cyberoperations and major defensive cyberoperations demand a narrative. Such narratives, though, do not come prepackaged. Cyberoperations lack precedents or much expressed declared intent to fall back on, and the normal human intuition about how things work in the physical world translates poorly into cyberspace. Because their effects and sometimes even their existence are not directly visible, the nature and ramifications of cyberoperations begs for explanation—generally by the target. Even the source of the attacks may be unclear and have to be claimed by the attacker or assigned by the defender.

The purpose of a cyberattack may lack obviousness. Two of the historical rationales for military operations are to seize something tangible or to destroy the adversary's ability to wage war. Cyberattacks

---

[1]   Tom Wolfe, *The Painted Word*, New York: Bantam, 1977.

cannot directly take anything *away* from others. Alone, a cyberattack can rarely disarm an adversary; its effects are almost always temporary and reversible.[2] Thus, if unaccompanied by physical force, its primary purpose is necessarily coercive or countercoercive: It sends a message or, more generally, attempts to get the target of the attack to do or not do something. At times, this something will be obvious, but misinterpretation is common. A few words can work wonders in conveying intent.

Narratives to Promote Control

The first rule of strategy is to make sure that one's strategists are in charge of events and not the other way around. The first rule of narration, correspondingly, is to support the first rule of strategy.

If, in fact, U.S. interests lie in quelling a crisis, then the last thing the leadership needs is to be pressed to greater crisis by hungry media and expedient politicians. To be sure, there will be circumstances under which such sentiment allows leaders to plead that they must have concessions from the attacker lest they be overwhelmed (a good-cop, bad-cop dynamic at play).[3] Such concessions then end the crisis. But there is risk in generating such sentiment only to find exploiting that sentiment prevents reaching a later modus vivendi.

---

[2] Stuxnet remains the only known cyberattack that actually broke something. If nothing else, it showed that, *if* equipment can be damaged by commands generated by digitized control systems, *and* these controls can be reprogrammed remotely, *and* the means to reprogram such controls are accessible to the outside world, then they might be damaged by cyberattack. Conversely, according to experts, such as Nancy Leveson (*SafeWare: System Safety and Computers*, Reading, Mass.: Addison-Wesley, 1995), software that can harm people and, by extension, break machines is fundamentally of poor design. The centrifuges destroyed by Stuxnet were also poorly monitored. There was very little human oversight on the floor (so that audible changes in rotation speed were not noticed) and no instrumentation monitors that were electronically separated from the controllers (observations confirmed in a conversation with Ralph Langner, an infrastructure security consultant).

[3] A state may also choose to exacerbate tensions as a way of getting domestic victims to clean themselves up and ensure that there will not be a repeat, but it then must come to terms somehow with the accused government—thereby raising the question about whether there might not be less risky ways of motivating system owners to do what they should do anyway.

The other path—playing down the crisis, at least initially, while facts are gathered and plans made—requires the right words. But it also requires considerable self-control over actions taken in the crisis. Consider the crisis scenario portrayed in *Cyber Shockwave,* a televised simulation of a cyberattack presented by the Bipartisan Policy Center.[4] The first instinct of the policymakers was to get ahead of the crisis by taking ownership of it; this they did by constantly pressing for new powers. Extraordinary powers, of course, require extraordinary circumstances to justify. Portraying a cyberattack in vivid colors highlights the heinous nature of the attackers. Many in the exercise showed irritation at Russia for having been the (unwitting?) home of the server from which the crisis emerged, and not jumping to help the United States find the ultimate perpetrator (and perhaps his support network). Portraying the crisis as something *a nation's* (our) *infrastructure owners* let break rather than something *an attacker* (they) did to *the nation* (us) puts the onus on (our) infrastructure owners to fix it. This would have colored the crisis differently and allowed the national command authority more flexibility in playing the crisis vis-à-vis other countries that may have been implicated. In this crisis, attribution came very early, perhaps unrealistically so. In the days and weeks it takes to restore service, the *domestic* crisis would be in the process of resolution, while the source and motivation of the attack may still be under investigation. If, at some later date, authorities conclude that a confrontation needs the backing of an aroused and angry citizenry, the attribution phase of the crisis provides the opportunity to encourage such sentiments.

A Narrative Framework for Cyberspace

States in search of consistent and credible narratives to explain their actions in a cybercrisis may want to present, preferably in advance, their fundamental posture toward what rules should govern individual

---

[4]   See Bipartisan Policy Center, "Cyber ShockWave," c. 2010.

and state behavior in cyberspace.[5] Such a posture may not necessarily conform to those rules that a state would want to have govern physical spaces.

Consider the following set of alternative cyberpostures, derived from a standard analytical trope, a two-by-two matrix, as depicted in Figure 3.1. The construct acts whether cyberspace should be treated as a commons. Note that it does not ask whether cyberspace is a commons, which it really is not. In the oceans and outer space, which *are* commons, two entities can collide with one another or at least interfere in each other's operational zone; interference is an issue also in spectrum. Hence the need for rules there. But, every part of cyberspace (except for long-distance spectrum) is owned and operated by a specific entity; with good management, collision or interference ought not to be an issue. Similarly, at the physical level, a hostile Asian state cannot interfere with traffic between the United States and Europe. At the syntactic level, however, such a possibility exists. An innocent-looking bitstream, allowed onto the physical infrastructure because it appears benign, can be malign enough to take out servers or routers; a DDOS attack can isolate and has isolated small countries.

One posture could be that cyberspace is *like* a global commons in the sense that it should be available for the unhampered use of all (criminals and criminal states aside) but governed by rules consistent with U.S. values. The posture says that the United States would be prepared to defend the status of cyberspace as such—much as the United Kingdom did for the ocean commons and as the United States is inching toward doing for outer space.[6]

A second posture, that cyberspace is a global condominium, is optimistic about an agreement but prepared to accommodate the vastly different values of other states. It is up to the world's major states to write rules for its usage and then cooperate in upholding such rules.

---

[5] The U.S. government's *International Strategy for Cyberspace*, released on May 16, 2011 (Obama, 2011), (1) chose to specify what values it sought, (2) called on other states to support them, and (3) reserved its right to carry out self-defense. But it did not argue that cyberspace was a commons as such.

[6] "Junk Science: Scientists Are Increasingly Worried About the Amount of Debris Orbiting the Earth," *Economist*, August 19, 2010.

Figure 3.1
Alternative Postures for a Master Cyber Narrative

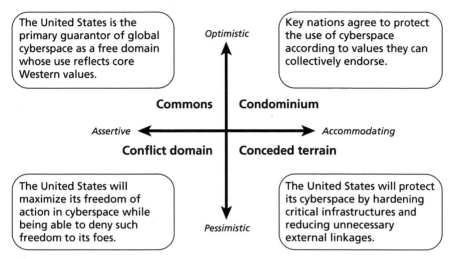

Optimistic

The United States is the primary guarantor of global cyberspace as a free domain whose use reflects core Western values.

Key nations agree to protect the use of cyberspace according to values they can collectively endorse.

Commons | **Condominium**

Assertive ←————————→ *Accommodating*

Conflict domain | **Conceded terrain**

The United States will maximize its freedom of action in cyberspace while being able to deny such freedom to its foes.

The United States will protect its cyberspace by hardening critical infrastructures and reducing unnecessary external linkages.

Pessimistic

RAND MG1215-3.1

Because, for instance, most states outlaw computer hacking, presumably all cooperative states will assist one another in suppressing it (traditional espionage aside). U.S. adoption of the condominium narrative means trading off a smaller say in the rules to get more help when enforcing them.

A third posture would reflect pessimism about a global accord but assert the U.S. ability to shape the medium: cyberspace as a conflict domain. Control over cyberspace would be deemed integral to the ability to defend a state and its allies against domination by other states, just as the power of the United States depends on the ability to control the air. Because the major powers are at peace with one another, and every state has a sovereign space it would control, a narrative of conflict ought to be in abeyance. But such a posture puts other nations on notice that the United States does not have to accept, in peacetime, cyberspace rules that might jeopardize its ability to defend itself there.

A fourth is pessimistic about agreement, conceding that no one nation, even the United States, can do much about cyberspace. Of the four narratives, this one is least likely to be voiced—except perhaps in the unlikely event that the United States is pestered by its friends to "do something" or even in the more unlikely event that the United States wishes to justify delinking many parts of the critical U.S. portion of cyberspace from that of the world beyond its shores.

The choice among these postures is not easy when each of them has at least some desirable features. The United States may want the help of other nations (condominium) to support U.S. values (commons) in cyberspace while retaining the right to dominate cyberspace if it has to (conflict domain) and conceding that, if it cannot, it has to be prepared to hunker down and protect itself (concession). Nevertheless, the failure to pick one posture and stick to it detracts from the narrative that a state has ideals that it is willing to hold to, even if occasionally inconvenient.

Advancing one or another posture colors how the United States would handle a global crisis and what immediate narratives the United States deploys when in a crisis. Consider, for instance, how the United States would justify assistance to Estonia and resistance to Russia after a hypothetical repeat and intensification of the 2007 attack. A U.S. posture that held cyberspace to be a commons would argue that defending cyberspace was called for irrespective of the geography of attack (just as attacks on non-U.S. satellites in geosynchronous equatorial orbits are a U.S. concern even though the United States does not lie on the equator). A condominium posture would lead the United States more to call on Russia to live up to its laws and act against the hackers; Russia's response would color whatever narrative the United States then chose. A posture that highlights cyberspace as a conflict domain would support a narrative that damage to Estonia, a NATO ally, would tempt others to test alliance networks, a prospect fraught with security implications. Finally, a true concession posture, although consistent with the United States helping Estonia recover, is inconsistent with taking action against Russia.

Victimization, Attribution, Retaliation, and Aggression

Cyberoperations whose effects are publicly felt need to be consistent with the stories that states tell to their citizens and to each other. These stories reflect the narrator's self-chosen status as a victim, an accuser, a retaliator, or an aggressor.

Victimization

If the damage from a cyberattack is clear, victimized states must decide how they wish to assign blame and how much they wish to play up the incident. Sometimes, as with corruption attacks in general or the Stuxnet attack in particular, the damage is not obvious and emerges slowly.

One option is to say nothing. Because cyberattacks are matters of deception rather than force, victims must, essentially, admit that their machines and they, by extension, were conned.[7] Perhaps they really were betrayed by their employees and vendors, but organizations and states bear responsibility for the people they hire and the systems they engineer. Perhaps they adopted a technology whose risks they did not fully understand.[8] There is no pride involved in being a victim. The embarrassment factor complicates the narrative of righteous victimization as a basis for indignation, particularly if the state was behind the curve in admitting the damage. With Stuxnet, Iran said nothing until the attack was revealed by others. Then it said that nothing went wrong. A few months later, it admitted that it had a problem but that the problem was over. Labeling Stuxnet as a vicious and damaging attack on the state of Iran that demands a response required changing the tenor of its characterization and hoping that its citizens had short memories.[9] In such a case, one role of narrative would be to divert attention from the poor practices that allowed the attack.

---

[7] In some cases, the embarrassment factor can be modulated. The target of a DDOS attack is not the one that was fooled, but DDOS attacks have limited effects. A criminal cyberattack that empties the accounts of hapless users also does not embarrass the state except insofar as the point of bank and related regulations is to protect consumers from themselves and put the burden on financial system operators.

[8] An attack carried out by a supposedly friendly state that has been given privileges on a major system and then betrayed that trust can easily give rise to justified fury but less embarrassment.

[9] In the early 1980s, the Soviet Union lost a gas pipeline because the electronic technology that it stole in order to control the pipeline had been corrupted precisely to cause such an

Shedding the shame is easier if the victimized state can direct the subsequent narrative away from the poor practices that allowed an attack and more on what the attack demonstrates about the intentions and moral capacity of the attacker. But "intent" is tricky. If the victim wishes to argue that a cyberattack, for instance, was prefatory to a military attack, it should have to make the case *before* the window of opportunity following a cyberattack closes. Even if the ordinary citizen may not realize that such a window exists, if the case is made *after* systems are restored, the intent to exploit the interim chaos while systems are down can point only to the attacker's broad plans ("just because we stopped them once does not mean they will stop trying") and not to any immediate threat.

Attribution

Attribution is accusation, and accusation is most credible as a story in which the cyberattack is a logical component of visible events. It must offer a credible motive based on the character of the state and what such a state is trying to achieve. The accused, unless it does not mind the accusation sticking,[10] will concoct an alternative narrative and, quite likely, will build it around the character of the accuser and how the accusation itself is a logical, or even necessary, component of the accuser's character.

Forensics alone may not carry the narrative. Although a few individuals will understand the forensics, the rest, even among the decisionmaking elite, will have to trust experts, which suggests a problem in letting the normally secretive intelligence community represent the nation's cyberwar expertise. Alas, clearer cases in the physical world still beget confusion: After all, the evidence on who carried out the September 11 attacks is largely unquestioned in the West, but half of

---

accident. To have started an international incident over the matter would have been to admit being a crook *and* a fool.

[10] Even though al Qaeda sought to polarize the Islamic world between it and the United States, Osama bin Laden initially denied complicity in the September 11 attacks, albeit not very strenuously or persistently. See, e.g., "Bin Laden Says He Wasn't Behind Attacks," CNN, September 17, 2001.

those polled in the Islamic world believed otherwise.[11] South Korea substantiated its claim that the March 2010 sinking of its naval vessel was an attack carried out by North Korea, but it remains to be seen how widely its evidence is believed in, say, China.[12]

Some stories can be built from what the attacker did afterward, especially if the cyberattacks had specific aims (apart from annoying their targets). What if a cyberattack disrupted some defense or intelligence capability, setting the stage for a kinetic military operation (e.g., put forces on a disputed island)? Would this constitute de facto admission that such a state carried out the attack? Or would the military operation be deemed opportunistic? However, if the act required preparation that could have started only *prior to the attack*, or the effects of the cyberattack would not have been apparent except to the victim *and the attacker*, then a better case for attribution exists.

Might the reactions of the accused attacker support the accusation? Maybe not: People and states, once accused, are naturally defensive whether innocent or not. Even a state's reluctance to open up its records for investigation may prove nothing; such acquiescence may be considered an unwise precedent.

Retaliation

Overt retaliation needs a separate justification. The retaliator has to make a statement not only about the wages of sin but also about the character of the sinner. Some nations will seek to broadcast ferocity in response to a successful attack. Others simply will not care what everyone else thinks. The rest, the United States included, will want to make retaliation fit some master narrative about who they are and what kind of rules they would like the world to run by.

Is *any* retaliation qua retaliation justified? With rare exceptions (e.g., the 1986 raid on Libya) recent punitive operations have been justified by specific operational ends: e.g., attacks on dual-use facilities,

---

[11] Andrea Stone, "Many in Islamic World Doubt Arabs Behind 9/11," *USA Today*, February 27, 2002.

[12] Joohee Cho, "'Obvious' North Korea Sank South Korean Ship," ABC News, May 19, 2010.

such as power plants or bridges in order to win wars, air strikes against surface-to-air missile (SAM) sites (e.g., the 1998 Desert Fox campaign against Iraq), or blockades to reduce supplies available to nations that misbehave (e.g., Israel's Gaza policy). The hurt was regarded as unsought or secondary.

Because retaliation limited to cyberspace cannot disarm, it can be justified only by some desired change in a state's behavior. A justification narrative, in such cases, must be robust enough to tolerate the wide difference between what may look proportional and what is actually achieved by the retaliation itself, which may vary widely from intentions. Thus, the retaliator may have to pretend that the range of planned effects produced matches the range of intended effects, lest it appear feckless in promising what it cannot hit or reckless in creating more effects than it wanted to—or both. Even if the effects cannot be precisely known, a certain rough justice may be communicated. If the source of the attack, for instance, comes out of the universities but the state is clearly behind the operation, then retaliation that targets the state's financial elites may seem misdirected; conversely, if the victim thinks that the attack emerged from organized-crime elements, then retaliation that targets the intellectual elite may seem similarly misdirected. In either case, the linkage between retaliation as a theater of morality ought to reinforce its use as a way of changing the state's behavior (whether it commanded the attackers or condoned their activities).

The target of retaliation will have its own counternarrative. Of course, it is innocent of the original attack, but, to prove the evil nature of the retaliator, it may also have to exploit the details of the retaliation. For example, a narrative that holds the retaliator to be the enemy of the local religion will be reinforced by any cyberattack on religious institutions—hence the dilemma if the retaliator suspects that the original attack *did* come from religious institutions, such as those whose schoolhouses trained the attackers.[13] Making the victim's task easier is the fact that the target of retaliation holds the lion's share of evidence

---

[13] Cyberspace, where nothing is directly visible, may also provide an opportunity for attacking oneself (without actually having to hurt one's own citizens) and blaming it on enemies in

of "who done it," and the target can easily argue for selective revelation by claiming that releasing details reveals too much about its sensitive infrastructure.

The public's ire against its own state for having brought forth retaliation by an unprovoked attack might also be deflected if the retaliation landed on a target *not* controlled by the state, such as a private bank. The aggressor state may focus blame on organizations that chose to expose their systems to the world—and hence the retaliator—without building in sufficient security. Such a counternarrative communicates the attacking state's refusal to be intimidated by retaliation, either directly (because it does not yield) or indirectly (because it need not accept the public's blame for the incident). To avoid such an argument, the retaliator may have to find targets that are the responsibility of the attacking state.

Aggression

The attacker's narratives can announce its strength rather than its innocence. It can argue, "We can hit, and we can take hits, and you can do neither." Such a narrative may emphasize the weakness of the target to cyberattack, hinting that states unable to defend their own military infrastructure from cyberattack should think twice about investing in high technology or, more broadly, should think twice about starting a fight. The attacker may warn other states not to associate with states that venture the targeted state's data and other assets into a domain it could not defend. In some cases, the message may be manipulated to include the source of the attack. If it appeared to be coming from an ally or an entity that provides services,[14] the whispered narrative may be, "do you trust them?" If it seemed to be coming from someone on the inside, a similar narrative may be, "given the incipient unrest in your country, can you even trust your own forces?"

---

circumstances in which exculpatory evidence (e.g., "our aircraft never flew near that target") is difficult to provide.

[14] Discovery of the Stuxnet worm caused Iran to arrest several people and may have soured Iran on working with Russians.

The extent to which a cyberattack supports a narrative of aggression meant to coerce others will depend on who these others are. A tank may intimidate in Bosnia largely because Europeans have narratives of war in which tanks are deciders. A similar tank in, say, Afghanistan may not work so well because, in Afghanistan narratives, tanks are easier to picture as sitting ducks. In the foreseeable future, no cyberattack can draw from a well of precedent for its images. A secondary consideration is whether there *are* similar precedents of which cyberattacks may remind potential victims.

Emollients: Narratives to Walk Back a Crisis

A special case of the narrative challenge arises when a state is accused of carrying out a cyberattack without evident reason for doing so. To wit, the cyberattack is not claimed, is not part of any coercive strategy, and is unassociated with kinetic activity, or even a crisis in the physical world. One state may act in a way it deems innocent, or at least legitimate, taking actions that are within the bounds of what it thinks it can do, only to find that its actions are misread, misinterpreted, or taken to be a signal that the other state never sent. From the perspective of the offended state, the innocence of the offending state may not be a given; it may be lying, asserting privileges to which it knows it has no right, or hiding a radical shift in its aims within the cloak of everyday behavior. Here, a crisis may be more likely when the target of the attack pressures the alleged perpetrator to yield the individual attacker, make recompense, back down, or do whatever else is appropriate.[15] This puts the onus on the alleged perpetrator to explain its actions if it wishes to tamp down the crisis. In this section, we look at a few of them in terms of what the accused might say and how the accuser may take things.

---

[15] As opposed to a crisis that stems from exploiting the consequences of a cyberattack.

"We Did Nothing"

China has responded to accusations with a variety of the following:[16] The accusation is irresponsible; tracing an attack to a Chinese server proves nothing because third-party attackers can hop through China (and sometimes do); and China, itself, is a victim of cyberattacks.[17] Outside of China, this response is regarded as stonewalling. Up until mid-2012,[18] the United States has been content to leave matters there, but it is not clear that the United States would do so following an incident comparable to the ones described in Chapter One.

As a general rule, the question of fault determination—what happened—eventually gets solved. Experience with faults in cyberspace suggests that the likelihood of reaching conclusions about their origin is at least as high as it is for faults in the physical world. But, these investigations can take time, which a crisis does not always afford.

The question of who attacked is empirical and may well get resolved one way or the other through the accumulation of incontrovertible facts—but not necessarily, much less in time to influence the course of the crisis. This raises the question of what states can do to build confidence among others that they are trying to resolve the crisis quickly by making it easier for others to determine that they really are innocent.

The prospect of two suspicious states trying to resolve what happened is fraught. The target would be understandably reluctant to let the presumed attacker's representatives explore their systems to determine what went wrong and whether the presumed attack was what the target claimed it was. The target may also be loath to reveal collected information on the attacker's modus operandi that would indi-

---

[16] See, e.g., Meghan Kelly, "Cyber Criminals Attack U.S. Chamber of Commerce, China Footing the Blame," *VentureBeat*, December 21, 2011.

[17] "Chinese officials have routinely denied the cyberspying, insisting that their own country also is a victim of such attacks" (Lolita C. Baldor, "US, China to Cooperate More on Cyber Threat," Associated Press, May 8, 2012).

[18] According to Siobhan Gorman, "U.S. Homes In on China Spying," *Wall Street Journal*, December 13, 2011, in late 2011, "U.S. officials met with Chinese counterparts and warned China about the diplomatic consequences of economic spying, according to one person familiar with the meeting."

cate that the attack used such a modus operandi—if such information were gathered by intelligence sources and methods.[19]

Consider two strategies, one intrinsic and the other extrinsic. The intrinsic strategy attempts to build confidence through the actions of the accused party. One element is to offer facts that prove innocence. Examples may include an overall bent to transparency, notably an investigative process that others trust to dig for facts (howsoever deeply into the nation's internal workings) and display the facts even if these facts are unflattering. Inviting the accusers to witness the investigation or, better yet, inviting them to conduct the investigation would be credible, but many states, understandably, are reluctant to have their citizens subject to the investigation of other states, something that violates many tenets of sovereignty. Furthermore, potentially hostile states may be overly eager to trace investigative trails through the national security bureaucracies of others, even if their odds of finding anything relevant to the case at hand are low. Perhaps something similar to the U.S. legal concept of discovery (the accuser gets to see what the accused state finds) may achieve a happy medium.

A second element in the intrinsic strategy is to take positions that would be very embarrassing if wrong, or to establish a policy that satisfies others that *individuals* caught stonewalling face severe repercussions. Clearly, states that wish to pursue such a policy ought to start before the crisis in order to establish a track record of honesty. The expressed statement that "we have nothing to hide," however, accompanied by indications that those who hide matters will suffer accordingly may fill in the gap. True, states can engineer more-sophisticated hiding techniques; however, the more complicated the dance, the greater the odds of slipping.

The extrinsic strategy calls on a neutral third party, one unassociated with any state, to carry out such an investigation. This, too, is tricky; the accuser cannot accept such an arrangement without admitting that it does not trust the accused party (of course, it may already

---

[19] During the Cuban missile crisis, the United States displayed imagery taken by formerly classified U-2 aircraft, but that was two years after one of them, with its surveillance camera, was captured by the Soviet Union.

have indicated as much), and the accused cannot accept it without admitting that its own investigations are unconvincing. The third party also has to be credibly chosen; cyberspace forensics is not a widespread skill, and many of its practitioners have links to the domestic or national security apparatus of one or another state, which may raise suspicions that the real purpose of the investigators is spying, not crime-solving.[20]

The search for an extrinsic approach to confidence-building has precedents, such as the 1959 Antarctic Treaty, which allows no-warning inspections of facilities. Its best value is establishing the principle of inspection; the precise analogy to a no-warning inspection (on servers in another country) does not get at the problem of criminal investigation, and the task of identifying servers by treaty in advance simply does not apply. Another precedent is the U.S. National Transportation Safety Board (NTSB),[21] which investigates accidents to understand the sequence of events coupled with system weaknesses in the vehicle that permitted the accident to occur, but it is specifically enjoined from assigning fault. NTSB reports are accepted as professional and disinterested in the United States, and the organization can command cooperation from vehicle owners. A similar mechanism may at least get partway to the truth in cyberattacks, especially if they are regarded as an induced accident, which is plausible from the perspective that a system cannot be attacked if it lacks vulnerabilities. The NTSB analogy may be usefully pushed one more step: If a foreign vehicle crashes in the United States, there may be a presumption that the presentation of its maintenance record can be compelled; a cyber equivalent may exist if countries agree to norms that require their ISPs to keep their customers' machines free of malware.

If states are truly interested in the truth, and the truth works against crisis exacerbation, then it may be useful to establish norms that govern how far accused states should go in fostering transparency.

---

[20] See, for instance, R. Jeffrey Smith, "U.N. Inspectors or Spies? Iraq Data Can Take Many Paths," *Washington Post*, February 16, 1998, p. A01.

[21] Which has overseas equivalents in Australia, Canada, and Europe.

"Well, At Least Not on Our Orders"

This stage, if it exists, may follow the accumulation of facts that indicate the source of the attack. The "they" in this context could refer either to those resident in the country or, worse, to rogue elements within the government itself.

Presumably, presentation of such an excuse presupposes that the state means to pursue those who did it, but this is not necessarily the case. The "patriotic hacker" argument asserts that the effects, which collectively might have crossed a threshold, may have individually been beneath notice, and it was only the uncoordinated or spontaneously self-coordinated action of citizens rightfully enraged by the actions of the target state that created the objectionable level of disruption. This argument applies only to certain types of incidents, such as flooding attacks. This argument seeks safety in numbers, not only to distinguish actionable from nonactionable events but also to plead the inability to prosecute people in such large numbers (and without obvious leaders) and hint that the action acquired its legitimacy from the numbers themselves (e.g., the action was somehow deserved because the people have so decided).

The rogue-actor argument contends that the state apparatus would like to act against the perpetrators but lacks the political power to do so: Think Hezbollah in Lebanon, or Inter-Services Intelligence (ISI) in Pakistan. Furthermore, the argument may continue, although overseas cyberattacks are, of course, serious, the rogue actors have done much worse internally. If the state could not summon the resources to suppress the rogue actors' internal crimes, what makes anyone think they could suppress the rogue actors over something clearly less consequential even (especially?) if it hurt foreigners. (Such an argument may backfire if the target of the cyberattack then comes to understand that it has to exacerbate the confrontation to raise the urgency of addressing the rogue faction.) A more plausible variant is for the state to argue that it cannot effectively investigate the rogue faction well enough to determine its culpability. Note that this argument presupposes a state willing to admit that it is weak; China and the United States, for instance, cannot use the faction argument very easily.

The not-us argument may also be used proactively as a way of managing the implications of an act. If a state were caught carrying out espionage against another state's power grid, the target may justifiably believe that the incident was a precursor to an attack that would accompany, say, a military operation. If, however, a rogue faction or a nonstate actor (e.g., a hacker for hire) that lacked reach into other state activities were responsible, the linkage between espionage and war would be much weaker. Therefore, the justification for the target to mobilize a response would be correspondingly weaker as well. More broadly, no operation by a rogue factor or a nonstate actor can be held to imply anything firm about a state's attitudes or intentions.

Unfortunately, the not-on-my-orders argument can backfire. Civilian leadership over militaries is not everywhere an established fact, and opacity of cyberoperations makes their civilian control even more difficult. Accordingly, a target state may not necessarily react calmly to the attacking state's excuse that it could not exercise (or would not exercise?) control over its cyberwarriors. It may reason that, whereas it had many ways of modulating the behavior of the attacking state, it lacked ways to modulate the behavior of the rogue faction and needed to acquire more, not least by reaching out and touching the rogue faction itself. The latter option may exacerbate the crisis.

Issues of C2 color the inferences that states make about the actions of other states. To what extent do the corporations in a state act as arms of the state itself? Many countries believe that companies, such as Microsoft, Google, and Facebook, are arms of the U.S. government and that their avid and energetic attempts to collect personal information on their customers to be fed to gigantic data-mining machines is just another form of espionage. To most American ears, this claim is preposterous. But, Americans, in turn, worry that Huawei, a Chinese manufacturer of telecommunication equipment, acts on behalf of the People's Liberation Army (PLA).[22] After all, its chief executive was a PLA officer (ignoring the number of U.S. corporations headed by former military officers). An organization with a Huawei router

---

[22] See, for instance, "Huawei: The Company That Spooked the World," *Economist*, August 4, 2012.

could find unknown software processes siphoning off critical information, despite the corporation's offer to show its source code to doubters (the eavesdropping features could be in the updates, doubters would retort). Chinese may find this claim just as preposterous—unless, of course, it is true.

Similar mistrust may affect how states read statements conveyed by members of the governing apparatuses of other states. When a Chinese general remarks that Los Angeles may be at risk if the United States gets too aggressive over Taiwan or another one suggests that China would go to war to protect Iran,[23] are they not speaking for China itself? After all, U.S. generals are not allowed to (or at least not supposed to) to speak publicly outside the bounds of their official position. Conversely, when a background source in the United States claims that the proper response to a cyberattack may be a cruise missile placed down the smokestack of a factory in the attacking country,[24] or a major presidential candidate argues in favor of starting a cyberwar against Iran, are they not speaking for the United States itself? Americans shrug such statements off as political froth.

Ultimately, these questions come down to whether one side has confidence in another side's ability to exercise C2 over its cyberforces or in each other's willingness to exert such C2.

---

[23] According to Stephanie Lieggi, "Going Beyond the Stir: The Strategic Realities of China's No-First-Use Policy," Washington, D.C.: Nuclear Threat Initiative, January 1, 2005, in 1996, the U.S. media reported that a Chinese military officer had, in the presence of former Assistant Secretary of Defense Charles Freeman, threatened to attack U.S. cities with nuclear weapons. Reports on the comments—often attributed to General Xiong Guangkai, although the identity of the Chinese official has never been confirmed by Freeman—often claim that the official threatened nuclear attack against Los Angeles if there were a conflict over Taiwan. And Matthew Robertson, "Chinese Admiral Threatens World War to Protect Iran," *Epoch Times*, December 6, 2011, updated December 22, 2011, reports, "according to a report in Press TV, a news network owned by the Iranian government, Chinese rear admiral and prominent military commentator Zhang Zhaozhong said, 'China will not hesitate to protect Iran even with a third world war'" (note that the source, *Epoch Times*, is associated with a dissident Chinese group).

[24] The quote is, "If you shut down our power grid, maybe we will put a missile down one of your smokestacks" (see Siobhan Gorman and Julian E. Barnes, "Cyber Combat: Act of War," *Wall Street Journal*, May 31, 2011).

"It Was an Accident"

The attacking state admits guilt but maintains that its actions were legitimate (e.g., espionage) even if its outcomes (e.g., disruption, corruption) were less so. The point is not only to argue that the punishment should fit the intended crime but that inferences made about the state using the act as evidence should be replaced by the far less alarming inferences that can be drawn from the intended act. This case requires some evidence that the attack could have resulted from one or two errors (no such argument, for instance, could be made for Stuxnet). States can also be legitimately blamed for authorizing incompetent people to carry out an operation that carried an unacceptable risk of damage.

If claims of such accidents are not just a smokescreen, the behavior of state agents in cyberspace may be usefully constrained by certain norms, just as the behavior of naval vessels is. During the Cold War, the United States and the Soviet Union experienced may incidents at sea that can be expected when one or both sides play too close to the line and neither communicates its intentions very clearly.[25] There may be analogies in cyberspace—maybe. Exactly how to specify them may be hard to say if the time required to negotiate and establish enforcement mechanisms exceeds the window during which such an accident is possible before periodic changes in the software environment render the whole topic moot. This window may be shorter than the time it takes to negotiate treaties. Concerns about the impact that rapidly spreading worms, starting with Nimda and Code Red in 2001 through Slammer in 2003, could have on the Internet were assuaged not through treaty, law, or regulation[26] but when Microsoft introduced Service Pack 2 to its XP operating system to correct systemic flaws in its Internet Information Server (IIS) software.

---

[25] See David Frank Winkler, *The Cold War at Sea: High-Seas Confrontation Between the United States and the Soviet Union*, Annapolis, Md.: Naval Institute Press, 2000.

[26] George W. Bush, *The National Strategy to Secure Cyberspace*, Washington, D.C.: White House, February 2003.

"This Is Nothing New"

States do have tacit understandings of what is and is not passable behavior among themselves, but such understandings do not cover all contingencies, especially novel ones. Too few cyberattacks have taken place to establish boundaries with any degree of precision, and the field is evolving quickly enough that a large percentage of activities will be unprecedented or at least have important novel elements. Analogies with physical space (e.g., what constitutes a sovereign domain) are not always drawn the same way by everyone. In addition, the line between what accords to precedent and therefore merits prima facie acceptance and what would establish a new precedent may be fuzzy; otherwise, say, U.S. constitutional law would not be as interesting as it is.

Protesting innocence by arguing that one or another action is legitimate is hardly the last word. Nor does it help that the offended state can credibly deny that it opposes such actions if it carries out such actions surreptitiously itself. Does the United States, for instance, have the right to establish a virtual embassy in a country in which it has no physical representation, if the attempt to do so violates the state's sovereign right (or so it is claimed) to monitor and potentially block communications with its citizens?[27] Does that state, in turn, have a right to block such communications, not only by limiting what its citizens can access but also by making such a site inaccessible to anyone (e.g., through DDOS attacks)?

Finally, the mad intersection between cyberattack, surveillance, circumvention, and intellectual property protection may be a source of unintentional crises. Many, perhaps most, computers in some countries use bootlegged software.[28] If a U.S. corporation were to introduce a "patch" that disabled such computers, the rationale would be under-

---

[27] This is a reference to U.S. attempts to establish a virtual embassy in Iran (see Kirit Radia, "Iran Blocks U.S. 'Virtual' Embassy Within 12 Hours of Launch," ABC News, December 7, 2011).

[28] According to Owen Fletcher and Jason Dean, "Ballmer Bares China Travails," *Wall Street Journal*, May 26, 2011, "Rampant piracy means Microsoft Corp.'s . . . revenue in China this year will only be about 5% of what it gets in the U.S., even though personal-computer sales in the two countries are almost equal, Chief Executive Steve Ballmer told employees in a meeting here."

standable; the cost, immense; the reaction, fierce; and the suspicions rampant.[29] More innocently, features inserted to conform to U.S. intellectual property law may disable certain functionalities (e.g., forms of file-sharing) on which users in other states may have counted to make their systems function as they want them to.

If silence signifies assent, then states may have little choice but to protest what they regard as unacceptable behavior lest such behavior be established as a norm. Sometimes the protest works, and sometimes not, and the new norms prove to be tolerable. During the Cold War, Soviet "fishing trawlers" would approach U.S. warships for purposes of electronic surveillance. These trawlers were initially deemed provocative and, as such, outside accepted norms. Later, they were accepted as the concomitant of operating in international waters.

In some cases, it is unclear what constitutes assent. For instance, there is a great deal of mischief in cyberspace—espionage from China, organized crime winked at by Russia—that the United States and its allies tolerate because the harm has been modest, attribution has been difficult, and the risks of making an issue of it have been daunting. Doubtless, there is U.S. behavior (e.g., support for the freedom to dissent) likewise tolerated by other states. Such tolerance may not last forever. There is growing impatience, as noted, with the (apparently) rising level of intellectual property theft via cyberspace, and there are indications that attribution for many of these attacks has become good enough to do something about.[30] If action is demanded and adequate compliance not forthcoming, a crisis may arise. Such crises are more easily resolved if the offending state has paid lip service to norms that it has broken (as is the case with hacking), and harder if these norms have yet to be established. Finally, never underestimate the ability of people, organizations, or states to shift the locus of the discussion from the act

---

[29] In 2008, "US information technology (IT) giant Microsoft launched a mechanism to blacken the screens of computers using counterfeit Windows. It's right to attack piracy, but the incident also exposed China's online vulnerability to high-tech intrusion from overseas" (Tang Lan, "Let Us Join Hands to Make Internet Safe," *China Daily*, February 7, 2012).

[30] Gorman, 2011.

being protested, to the presumptive, unfair, discriminatory, or hostile act of protestation itself.

"At Least It Does Not Portend Anything"

A crisis can start from an incident or action that, in isolation, deserves neither condemnation nor attention but signifies something larger—notably, a shift in attitude on the scale from benign to no-holds-barred hostile. In some cases, the other side is left perplexed, and crisis management in such a case is a matter of explanation and demonstration to the contrary. For instance, Chinese observers have regarded U.S. Department of Homeland Security (DHS) Cyber Storm exercises as a way of making the United States invulnerable to cyberwarfare, the better to attack others with impunity. The establishment of U.S. Cyber Command (USCYBERCOM) is viewed as a declaration of the U.S. right to use offensive cyberwar against others even though 80 to 90 percent of its efforts are defensive. The U.S. *International Strategy for Cyberspace*,[31] with its sometimes timorous language on deterrence (but with much stronger language on cyberespionage), was regarded in some quarters as a warlike document.[32]

Perhaps the state that acted was sending a message, but, given the tendency toward worst-case assessment coupled perhaps with mirror-imaging, the number of received hostile messages is likely to exceed the number of sent messages. The message's recipients may not always be open about the thing to which they are reacting; when they say as much, they could be whining for public consumption. Conversely, if the acting state offers enough emollient statements, the only conclusion the target states will receive is that it did not mean to signal the public—which hardly proves that it is does not signify hostility. Perhaps its messaging is esoteric; perhaps it would rather hide its intent with such messages.

---

[31] Obama, 2011.

[32] Adam Segal, "Chinese Responses to the International Strategy for Cyberspace," *Asia Unbound*, May 23, 2011.

In this regard, cybercrises resemble any other crises, exacerbated by the difficulty of understanding what actions in cyberspace predispose which moves in the real world.

Broader Considerations

Crises may be stoked by the misperception that cybersecurity is a zero-sum game: One state's security is purchased at the expense of another. If so, any positive change in cybersecurity by one side must be viewed with suspicion by another. This assumption is common in judging, say, the capabilities of armies and navies or the possession of land and waterway chokepoints, but, although the purpose of armies and navies is to fight wars, cybersecurity is just ancillary to these ends (and only if the systems made secure belong to militaries). A better analogy may be safety: Improving the safety features of ships does not imperil other navies as much as it eases the fears of sailors, but it is possible that all ships can be made safer and all sailors better off. The corollary belief that a state, by securing its civilian infrastructure, can therefore attack others in cyberspace with impunity rests on two improbable assumptions. The first is that it can actually (and provably) achieve such security; no one believes that such security is possible for any state that maintains networks, at least with today's information system architecture. The second is that states have no other way of responding except in kind.

A reasonable approach to walking back a crisis is to coolly analyze what the perpetrator hopes to achieve by the operation, incident, or action that would precipitate it.[33] Does it gain the attacker anything? Does it change the boundaries of what is acceptable? Most urgently, does it make a subsequent military attack easier (and, if so, over what time period does the advantage last)? If the target cannot determine whether any broader objective is enhanced by the action, then it can

---

[33] This is particularly important when analyzing a series of seemingly unrelated incidents with no obviously common feature. The hoary argument that the adversary is employing a subtle series of small attacks that collectively are designed to have a large effect should be held in abeyance until a plausible story can be concocted which explains *how* such attacks can foster a coherent end. Analogies to the game of Go are not helpful in describing attacks whose effects erode rapidly once discovered and corrected.

grant itself the luxury of treating the incident in isolation rather than as a precursor to or a signal of something greater ahead that must be vigorously opposed prior to its birth.

Signals

Thus far, we have discussed how narratives and dialogues can help manage cybercrises. Does signaling have a role in the management of cybercrises? Signaling uses actions to communicate seriousness. It was often employed in the Cold War. The United States signaled seriousness to the Soviet Union in 1948, during the Berlin blockade, by sending B-29s to the UK. In the U.S.-Soviet near-confrontation during the 1973 October War, President Richard Nixon signaled to Soviet leader Leonid Brezhnev by raising the status of U.S. forces to defense condition (DEFCON) 3, "a signal sufficiently clear that it never had to be mentioned in formal messages between the two."[34] During the Sino-Vietnam war, the Chinese air force tried to "to fly as many sorties as possible over the border airspace when the ground assaults started in order to deter the Vietnamese air force from taking action against China."[35] An oft-cited (perhaps apocryphal) tale has the United States reacting to its discovery that Soviet submarine forces were arrayed close to the East Coast by rebasing bombers toward Thule, Greenland. This signaled U.S. displeasure and put the Soviet Union on notice that its actions were observed, interpreted as hostile, and reacted to.

The efficacy of signaling depends, in large part, on its acceptance of a something *as* a signal. A state sending a chunk of its fleet to a trouble spot in the 19th century was universally regarded as a signal of seriousness,[36] but perhaps the reason it was regarded as a signal was the

[34] Yaacov Bar-Siman-Tov, "The Arab-Israeli War of October 1973," in Alexander L. George, ed., *Avoiding War: Problems of Crisis Management*, Boulder, Colo.: Westview Press, 1991, pp. 342–367, p. 356.

[35] Xiaoming Zhang, "China's 1979 War with Vietnam: A Reassessment," *China Quarterly*, Vol. 184, 2005, pp. 851–874, p. 862.

[36] Richard Smoke, *War: Controlling Escalation*, Cambridge, Mass.: Harvard University Press, 1997, p. 165.

confidence that others would regard it so, as well. In cyberspace, there is no basis for such confidence, and, until one emerges on its own, no reason to believe that such a basis can be ipso facto created.

Why signal when words can convey the same message? During the Cold War, to be sure, U.S.-Soviet state-to-state communications were indirect: The Hot Line did not exist until 1963. Using public communications may have engendered mutual contests in posturing, complicating mutual accommodation later. These days, communications are everywhere.

Another historical reason for signaling was to send the other side's leadership a message that only it could see. In the physical world, ubiquitous surveillance makes such discrimination much more difficult, but, in cyberspace, the prospects are better: Offensive actions may be visible only to their targets; defensive actions may be visible only to those exploring the relevant system deeply enough to notice the difference. But, although Soviet surveillance systems that revealed B-52s in Thule, for instance, would likely have led to an important message to the Soviet premier, it is unclear whether such a high-value asset in the physical world has its counterpart in cyberspace. Perhaps, the more critical the system, the more effort is put into its defense, thus, the more impenetrable it is, and the harder it is for states to sneak a message in there—but the stronger the signal if they can.

Yet, signaling serves another function that mere words do not. Talk is cheap and, being cheap, may not be taken seriously. Actions—such as stationing forces forward or canceling troop leaves—are more expensive. They convey a seriousness that words do not, and so does putting oneself in a position that would make retreat difficult if a crisis was not resolved.

How would the United States, for instance, tell others something that they did not already know and of which they were not already aware? For instance, if the United States responded to a flagrant cyber-crime by starting an investigation, doing so would not signal very much: Everyone expects it to do so. Responding to a flagrant cyber-crime by starting a federal investigation and conspicuously pulling resources away from other investigations and other agencies, though, would signal that the United States is quite displeased. The action may have been taken because of such displeasure, or it may have been taken to signal such displeasure. Ironically, the less that people think that it was meant as a signal, the stronger the signal it would be; it would be less likely to be perceived as show.

The correspondence between a signal's intent and its effect has to be carefully watched. Prior expectations matter. Potential attackers, for instance, will always have some idea, however well- or ill-grounded, of how a state will react to being attacked. In some cases, what a state says ("we stand eight feet tall") may not necessarily discourage attackers ("oh, we thought you were ten feet") more than silence would have.[37]

So, what can a state expect to gain from broadcasting the various ways in which it has prepared for cybercrises? Consider the following:

- What about better defenses to indicate that a state expects an attack and it is ready—so ready that attacks on it are likely to be futile, perhaps risky? Good defenses may be interpreted as a rational response to circumstances, such as a newly revealed threat or as an incidental response (e.g., the resources for defense are unexpectedly freed up, new technology becomes available, the new security chief has different priorities). Conversely, if the visible defenses were too burdensome to be maintained easily for long periods, then their existence sends a stronger signal.
- What about baring teeth? As oft noted, one cannot really reveal specific cybercapabilities without putting them at risk; the same is true for using them, even against third parties. A state could conspicuously hire more hackers for temporary use, but, because hackers need some familiarity with the target to be effective, this would not say anything about the short term. A state could also delegate authority downward or authorize hack-back attacks as a way of signaling that a state was prepared to defend itself even at

---

[37] Sometimes, signaling and operational deception can be antithetical. Chinese operational security just prior to China's intervening in the Korean War (late 1950) reduced the fidelity of its signal that it would not tolerate a UN presence too close to the Chinese border (Lebow, 1981, p. 149).

the risk that a crisis could get out of hand more easily.[38] Similarly, a state could allow its hackers to use techniques or targets that were hitherto forbidden.

- What about making certain targets *more* vulnerable? This would be akin to offering hostages and indicates that a state expects another state not to take advantage of its vulnerability. Unfortunately, it is not clear how to do this without empowering third-party hackers as well.
- How would a state convey that it considers certain targets off-limits? Again, it could create hostages—e.g., a state that puts a large amount of money into another state's stock market may convey its lack of interest in hacking the latter's financial markets.[39]

Ambiguity in Signaling

The case for caution in signaling exists because signals that emanate from what one does rather than what one says can be as or even more ambiguous in cyberspace than they are in physical space. To take an analogy from the old Cold War era, consider how others may react to a state that has started construction of a fall-out shelter program.

It is prepared. That is, having taken a cold hard look at the threat, it deems a fallout shelter program appropriate and wants to convey that it can control the losses it might suffer from a nuclear war and hence the degree of coercion that a threat can produce.

It is scared. Hitherto, it imagined that the odds of an attack were low or that the damage was bearable. It had confidence that its nuclear forces would absolutely deter war. Reassessment suggests that earlier confidence was misplaced.

It is on the warpath. As with the previous case, it perceives nuclear conflict as growing more likely, not because it deems the enemy more

---

[38] Akin to the argument made in Thomas C. Schelling, *The Strategy of Conflict*, Cambridge, Mass.: Harvard University Press, 1960, pp. 187–204.

[39] This example is not perfect: Hacking stock markets affects trades more than assets, and the money can be withdrawn just before the fur flies.

aggressive or capable but because it has reassessed the necessity of a nuclear confrontation. Building says, "we are about to become aggressive *because* we are protected."

These three messages are not necessarily mutually exclusive. A state may view its foes with new alarm, conclude that they are about to start something, and decide to preempt their coercion by accelerating its own capability and baring some teeth.

Now carry over this logic into cyberspace. The United States recently established USCYBERCOM. What might this convey to others?

It is prepared. Cyberspace is becoming a growing facet of warfare at every level, and it would be prudent to develop defensive and offensive capabilities to ensure that others do not dominate this new domain.

It is scared. The United States is increasingly aware that its vaunted superiority in conventional conflict—network-centric warfare—may be undermined if its military networks can be attacked by those too weak to match it on the conventional battlefield. Thus, the United States must quickly shore up its defenses and, following Gen James E. Cartwright, develop an offensive capability to ensure that no nation attacks the United States in cyberspace with impunity.[40]

It is on the warpath. The United States, home of the information revolution, is extending its wide technological lead over other countries by creating a new form of warfare that can defeat other nations without even having to show up to fight.

Again, these messages are not mutually exclusive and, like other interpretations of U.S. actions, are likely to be perceived differently by domestic audiences than by international ones, and there will be differences between one foreign country and the next. Furthermore, even intelligent foreigners misread how the United States works, and

---

[40] On March 21, 2007, James E. Cartwright, then commander of U.S. Strategic Command (USSTRATCOM) testified to the U.S. House of Representatives Committee on Armed Services, "History teaches us that a purely defensive posture poses significant risks. . . . When we apply the principle of warfare to the cyber domain, as we do to sea, air, and land, we realize the defense of the nation is better served by capabilities enabling us to take the fight to our adversaries, when necessary, to deter actions detrimental to our interests."

vice versa. Chinese observers, for instance, have expressed considerable unease at the DHS series of preparedness exercises, Cyber Storm, because they are thought to presage U.S. aggressiveness. This perception is inexplicable to anyone knowledgeable about DHS—but no less real for that.

To date, the United States has not generated a master narrative to accompany the establishment of USCYBERCOM, although many top defense and other national security officials have commented on the topic. Perhaps there is no such narrative; much of what goes on within bureaucracies reflects a struggle for power and is not meant to convey anything to anybody on the outside. Nevertheless, this will not be the last such action by the United States or any other country that may have others scratching their heads about what the United States "meant by that."[41] Although not every move is part of a narrative, it probably cannot hurt to ponder what others may infer from such actions.

Signaling Resolve

For years, Japan and China both claimed the Senkaku or Diaoyu Islands. In September 2010, the Japanese arrested a Chinese fisherman venturing too close to those islands and ramming Japanese vessels patrolling them. Under Chinese pressure, Japan released the fisherman, but, when pressed to apologize, Japan refused. The Chinese were said to be "testing Japan's resolve to back its territorial claims in the East China Sea."[42]

Is there a similar way to signal resolve in matters of cyberspace? A great deal depends on what a state has claimed as its due in that medium. If a state draws a line (e.g., "we will respond to cyberattacks," "we hold certain types of cyberespionage to be a hostile act," "we will not tolerate sites that host malware"), it commits itself to defending its claims if challenged. Otherwise, similar (indeed, all other) claims lose

---

[41] Supposedly, upon hearing of a diplomat's death, another diplomat—possibly Charles Maurice de Talleyrand-Périgord, more likely Prince Klemens Wenzel von Metternich—was supposed to have asked, "I wonder what he meant by that?"

[42] Martin Fackler, "Japan Asks China to Pay for Damages," *New York Times*, September 26, 2010.

credibility. Conversely, if it makes no claims, there is nothing about which to be resolute, hence little to signal.

Is there a cyberspace analogy to placing assets in harm's way? Traditionally, this signaled not only the readiness to use such assets but the intention to defend them. At first glance, *all* systems are in harm's way wherever they sit. Perhaps making a system more vulnerable by exposing it to a broader community—such as from air-gapped networks to Internet-connected networks—might signal such intent. Yet, doing so does not make a system easier to use for military operations, unless these operations somehow entail gathering the general public into the cause. At this juncture, such a move may well confuse rather than signal others.

Can signaling be used to warn others away from attacking certain classes of assets? Consider a standoff over disputed islands. The United States and a regional peer monitor each other to make sure that neither side gets the jump in assuming control over such property. Then the regional peer hacks into U.S. monitors. Perhaps, at that point, a signal that taking down monitors does not help manage crises may be given by hacking into something outside of the theater, where the stakes are larger.

As in so many of these cyber dilemmas, showing certainty in the face of doubt may be more important than showing courage in the face of fear. States get into trouble—or, more likely, think they have gotten into trouble—by not responding to salami tactics, in which small violations are tolerated, the cumulative effect begins to pinch, and the state realizes that it neglected to establish a clear line to demarcate tolerable from intolerable violations. Its reactions at a violation that looks similar to those that it ignored catch the violator off-guard, which leads to an unpredictable set of results. Unfortunately, even clear lines are easy to cross.

States also get into trouble if they cannot remember, or choose to forget, the history of earlier signals. If a state had signaled a red line in the past and failed to respond to violations of it, then other states may discount all future red lines. An added complexity in cyberspace is that two states may have different views of what constituted a crossed red line. One state that sees an intrusion into its natural gas networks may conclude that the only plausible motive was intelligence preparation of the battlefield prefatory to an attack, while the attacker may believe that it was only gathering intelligence for its own use (e.g., how such pipelines are managed), so its actions crossed no red line and it cannot understand the sharp response. The reverse is also possible: The attacker crosses a red line. The target is unaware that it did and so fails to respond. The attacker concludes that such red lines are not meant to be taken seriously.

Signaling resolve may mean, at least, signaling the intent and the requisite resources to measure events in cyberspace accurately and quickly. This not only is a prerequisite to effective action but also indicates that such information is being collected for a reason. Only with confidence in findings can one begin to signal resolve—to say the state intends to react—before it reaches the point at which the state must respond to maintain its credibility.

Signaling That Cybercombat Is Not Kinetic Combat

Should states convey their intention to limit a cybercrisis to cyberspace, and forswear escalation into kinetic combat? Would it mean regarding escalation from cyberspace to physical space as a new declaration of war? Or would signaling as much make the world safe for cyberwar?

A state may hope that the unspoken yet palpable fear of escalation into violence among its foes would restrain them from making hostile moves—only to find itself in a cybercrisis that, by its existence, proves that the implied threat of escalation did not discourage such moves. At that point, the state's primary focus would be containing the crisis— just as members of the Cold War NATO wanted the Soviet Union to believe that a conventional confrontation might go nuclear but, having found themselves in such a confrontation anyway, wanted to assure themselves that it would not.

Ways of signaling such a stance may be to (1) state as much, (2) conspicuously decouple strategic cyberoperations from noncyber-operations, or (3) point out that, in the wake of a cybercrisis, kinetic forces are not being put on a higher alert or are, in fact, being withdrawn into training. If the foe would otherwise think that suspicious or malicious behavior in cyberspace presaged kinetic combat, such signals may have their desired calming effect. If, however, the crisis began in other ways (e.g., spontaneously, perhaps by accident, or by the foe's deliberate sparking a crisis), then the value of the signal would have everything to do with how the foe reads the attempt to create a firebreak. If the foe believed that the declaring state really did not want a kinetic fight, then the latter's declaring as much tells no one anything. If the foe believed that the state was prepared for violence but declined to engage in it, it may read the declaration as deescalatory. Conversely, an aggressive foe might take such a declaration as evidence that, contrary to what it may have thought or feared, the target state really was not ready for violence. In that case, the attacker may believe that it can gain something by using force or stepping up cyberattacks; against such a foe, perhaps no crisis management would work anyway. Or such a stance may convey that the state was confident enough in its ability to dominate the proverbial escalation ladder at all rungs and could afford to declare a firebreak in the interests of peace. In the latter case, unless the foe were aggressive, it may conclude that it would be better off settling earlier rather than later, especially if it thought that such confidence suggested that its rival knew something the attacker did not. Finally, the foe may conclude that the state was playing to the bleachers (that is, shaping the actions to appeal to onlookers), as if to say that, whatever escalation ensued, regardless of how murky the onset, it was not at fault.

Conclusions

In war, hard physical reality is thought to trump the nice lies that people tell about it, but this was never completely true about physical combat, and it is far less true about cybercombat, in which the elements of reality—causes, but also effects—are difficult to determine. Even were the facts clear, their interpretations are not; even when both are clear, decisionmakers and opinionmakers may not necessarily understand them.

As people gain savvy about cyberspace, these narratives necessarily must become more sophisticated and nuanced. Until hard-won sophistication is gained, states, nonstate actors, and partisans on all sides have a great opportunity to make something of nothing or vice versa. If cyberwar becomes more consequential, look for states to avail themselves of such opportunities more often. Narratives become tools of crisis management.[43] Part of the strategy of interpretation is concocting narratives in which events take their designated place in the logical and moral scheme of things: "we're good, you're bad," "we're strong and competent, unless we have stumbled temporarily because of your evil." The stories told in crisis benefit from broader precrisis narratives that reflect the broad ethical values to which a state adheres as its attitude toward cyberspace.

Dialogues are another useful aspect of managing crises, particularly when the incidents that might spark a crisis appear unrelated to any military or strategic operation that the attacker is carrying out. The attacker may offer explanations (or denials); the attacked may then indicate whether they offer sufficient excuse.

---

[43] An interesting case of a narrative, albeit from the corporate world, might be Sony's. In mid-April 2011, Sony had to take down its PlayStation® Network (PSN) in the wake of a hack using what the corporation admitted was a known but apparently unpatched vulnerability (Elinor Mills, "Expert: Sony Attack May Have Been Multipronged," *CNET*, May 18, 2011). Sony took most of a week before it acknowledged that PSN was offline (Erica Ogg, "PlayStation Network Outage: 6 Days and Counting," *CNET*, April 26, 2011a). Sony was also initially unable or reluctant to reveal whether credit card or other personal information was taken; said the senior director of corporate communications, "Our efforts to resolve this matter involving re-building our system to further strengthen our network infrastructure . . . it [is] worth the time necessary to provide the system with additional security" (Chris Morris, "Hackers Take Down Sony's PlayStation Network," CNBC, April 25, 2011). Opinions varied on how sophisticated the attack was, with observers calling it tantamount to script kiddie work ("as simple as grabbing the tools and going after Sony"), while the corporation characterized it as "a very sophisticated attack." Apologies and offers of compensation followed within two weeks (Erica Ogg, "The PlayStation Network Breach [FAQ]," *CNET*, May 3, 2011b). After service was restored, Sony underplayed the incident, with its president observing, "Nobody's system is 100 percent secure . . . this is a hiccup in the road to a network future" (Don Reisinger, "Sony: PSN Difficulties a 'Bump in the Road,'" *CNET*, June 23, 2011), adding, when challenged on Sony's slowness in alerting customers, "there is no precedent for this in people's experience . . . most reports now seem to indicate that we acted very quickly and very responsibly" (Erica Ogg, "Sony: PSN Back, but No System Is 100 Percent Secure," *CNET*, May 17, 2011c). A month later, it was alleged that Sony had laid off employees in a unit responsible for network security two weeks prior to the attack ("Sony Laid Off Employees Before Data Breach," Reuters, June 23, 2011).

Signaling, a staple of the Cold War, may have less of a role to play in cyberspace, largely because, without explicit narrative, subtle signals could be misread among the confusing ends and means of cyberspace operations. That noted, others may treat U.S. actions as signals of their own. It would seem a worthwhile endeavor to anticipate such inferences and use narratives to align what U.S. actions convey and what U.S. strategy demands be conveyed. More broadly, U.S. combatant commanders ought to understand that narratives and, to a lesser extent, signals correlate a nation's actions in cyberspace with its overall policy objectives. If, presumptively, a nation's kinetic actions also reflect its policy objectives, then cyberactivities and kinetic activities should be correlated with one another.

CHAPTER FOUR

Escalation Management

Once a crisis has blossomed into conflict, crisis management becomes escalation management. The success of escalation management depends on the fact that both sides would prefer less disruption and violence rather than more of it—but not necessarily before they make their point to one another. At the very least, both sides share an interest in keeping control over what breaks out rather than ceding control to fate, the passions of warriors, the intrigues of factions, or third parties.

Admittedly, escalation in cyberspace remains a speculative topic. Few government officials have declared their red lines. The cyber equivalent of Herman Kahn's *On Escalation*[1] is yet unwritten. Not only do we lack a discrete metric for cyberwar, there is no good way to measure the proportionality of various cyberattacks systematically and consistently (e.g., "this act is more heinous or dangerous than that act").

After a quick review of escalation motives, this chapter covers three topics: (1) the risks of escalation associated with cyberattacks in various contexts, (2) third-party escalation, and (3) the difficulties of controlling escalation using tit-for-tat logic. Afterward, we examine escalation narratives that each side may offer and then issues associated with the C2 of cyberwarriors to implement escalation management. The chapter's context is a conflict in which cyberattacks matter in their own right, rather than being simply one more way to prosecute a target already threatened by kinetic means.

---

[1] Herman Kahn, *On Escalation: Metaphors and Scenarios*, Praeger, 1965.

Motives for Escalation

Those who would manage escalation by exercising self-restraint and persuading adversaries to do likewise should start with a sense of what the other hopes to get from unilateral escalation—that is, crossing some hitherto uncrossed red line.

A primary purpose of escalation is to gain military advantage.[2] Yet, a thinking combatant will recognize that, because escalation begets escalation, the military advantage from escalating will have to trump whatever military disadvantage arises when the adversary does likewise.

Calculating net advantage is tricky. The presumption that the adversary will escalate one level in response to a one-level escalation may fail if the adversary calculates that it loses on that round and thereby raises the stakes.[3] After two rounds, the advantages to the escalating side may disappear while the pain does not. In cyberspace, such calculations are particularly complex. Thresholds have yet to be established, or even described in common words. Worse, although each side can recognize the vulnerability of another after having scoped it, recognizing one's own vulnerability, and hence susceptibility to retaliatory cyberescalation, is inherently difficult:[4] If one were already aware of such vulnerabilities, chances are that they would have been already

---

[2] For a richer treatment, see Morgan et al., 2008, especially the first few chapters.

[3] Albert Wohlstetter and Richard Brody, "Continuing Control as a Requirement for Deterring," in Ashton B. Carter, John D. Steinbruner, and Charles A. Zraket, eds., *Managing Nuclear Operations*, Washington, D.C.: Brookings Institution, 1987, pp. 142–196, posits a hypothetical conflict with the Soviet Union circa 1985 that attacks NATO's southern flank with nuclear weapons to shatter the alliance. NATO concludes that it lacks a comparably good nuclear target that would have a similar effect, so it escalates to find its own sweet spot, which, by definition, is a sour spot for the Soviet Union, prompting it to counterescalate, and so on.

[4] One can parameterize certain types of vulnerabilities (e.g., the likelihood that a user has a compromised machine) statistically, but many of the nastiest attacks do enough damage if they succeed but once.

fixed.[5] It is thus easy for one side to argue that the *net* effect of escalation is positive because of inherent asymmetries in knowledge.

A secondary purpose of escalation is to signal seriousness, both to one's own side and to the other. To one's own side, it is a signal of support. A state that sends its military to fight and die in a theater is saying that it is willing to risk the adversary escalating to attacking the homeland in order to pursue military goals in theater. To the other side, escalation can say, "cut it out or someone is going to get hurt"; it can convey, for instance, that cyberespionage has reached a point at which the pain is tantamount to that of a cyberattack. If cyberescalation supports a theater military operation, it may communicate that the outcome of such a conflict matters a great deal.

A third purpose is to demonstrate one's power: "we can do this to your systems despite your best efforts to keep us out; now, do you trust them?" A related purpose is to carry out a contest of pain (or perhaps a contest in risk-taking, per Schelling's argument in *Arms and Influence*[6]). This presumes something called *escalation dominance*—the ability to outmatch one's foe at all levels of escalation.

A fourth purpose is to test the temper of opponents: How far are they willing to go? Are they rational and measured or irrational and erratic? An escalatory move may be tried to see how opponents would react. The advantage of doing so in cyberspace is that it provides *some* insulation against overreaction in the real world. But the value of such a test assumes that the same personality patterns that manifest themselves in cyberwar will manifest themselves similarly in physical (kinetic) war. Those that use cyberattacks to ping the other side have to contend with *four* sources of error if the response comes back by means of a cyberattack: (1) the difference between the intended attack

---

[5] This assumes that the government can fix vulnerabilities in infrastructure systems it does not own—an unwarranted assumption in peacetime, but plausible in wartime if such vulnerabilities threatened the war effort.

[6] Thomas C. Schelling, *Arms and Influence*, New Haven, Conn.: Yale University Press, 1966.

and its effect,[7] (2) the difference between the effect and its perception by the target, (3) the difference between the target's intended response and the effect it had, and (4) the difference between the actual effect of the target's response and how it was perceived by the original perpetrator (which is a problem both of measurement and of correlating the response to the original impulse). To this one can add miscalculation on the attacker's part about how the adversary will respond and the latter's miscalculations in response. The real signal may get lost in the noise of all the echoes, as illustrated in Figure 4.1.

Does Escalation Matter?

Our treatment assumes that states do have a positive interest in controlling their adversaries' use of cyberattacks and are willing to curtail their own use to that end. Here, we pause and ask, how much difference *is* there between a no-holds-barred cyberwar campaign and a

Figure 4.1
Sources of Imprecision in Tit for Tat

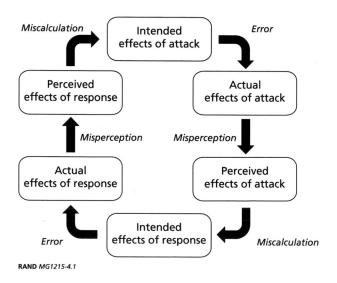

RAND MG1215-4.1

---

[7]   Or, if one is measuring the response from the "actual" effect of the test cyberattack rather than the intended effect, the error may come from the difference between the attacker's perception of the effect and the actual effect.

modulated cyberwar campaign? Violent war features very wide bands. Without war, a state's greatest worry about losing its citizens to violence is crime. By contrast, a nuclear-armed peer could kill everyone and break everything. There is a lot of scope for escalation within that band.

Now consider cyberwar. In today's environment, cybercrime is constant, with an annual cost to the United States in the billions of dollars and a plausible premise that, if a system with requisite vulnerabilities has something worth stealing, theft *will* take place and sooner rather than later. Because the general noise level is high in cyberspace, any retaliation that merits notice as such has to be loud. So the bottom is quite high.

The top end may be low, relative to conventional, much less nuclear, war. As noted, no one has yet been killed in a cyberattack, and there is scant indication that a full-blown attack could kill as many as a normal year's flu epidemic.[8] The most—commonly cited worst-case scenarios concern attacks on power companies that succeed in damaging a great deal of equipment, but extrapolating from Idaho National Laboratory's Aurora experiment or even Stuxnet to such a scenario is quite a stretch (safety and control considerations suggest that confused power equipment default to shutting down rather than damaging itself or other equipment).[9] Similarly, there is little basis for knowing how much damage can arise when modern process control and financial systems fail, or how well timely and intelligent human intervention can mitigate such costs. Similarly, there is little evidence of how much operators can damage their own equipment if they are misled by monitors that have been deliberately corrupted. Whether infrastructures have weaknesses that no one has seen yet to exploit but whose effects could be sharp and hard to fix remains unknown. All one knows is

---

[8] Roughly 6,000 per year, based on Centers for Disease Control and Prevention statistics from winter 1976–1977 through winter 2006–2007 (Centers for Disease Control and Prevention, "Estimates of Deaths Associated with Seasonal Influenza: United States, 1976–2007," *Morbidity and Mortality Weekly Report*, Vol. 59, No. 33, August 27, 2010, pp. 1057–1062).

[9] See Jeanne Meserve, "Sources: Staged Cyber Attack Reveals Vulnerability in Power Grid," CNN, September 26, 2007.

what has happened so far. By the standards of conventional warfare, the damage has not been terribly impressive—so far.

Perhaps the real reason to control cyberescalation is that matters may not end in cyberspace. One side may see that cyberattacks on targets that *were* off-limits to kinetic attack legitimize a kinetic attack on comparable targets: If cyberattacks on a sensitive system put lives at risk, why are they different from a kinetic attack that puts the same lives at risk? So, should targets considered off-limits from a physical attack also be off-limits from a cyberattack *that offers the potential of similar collateral damage*? A state hit by a devastating cyberattack may conclude that, like Indiana Jones, it is tired of getting cut with cyberknives and whip out its kinetic pistol. Such a reaction would trade the limited risks of cyberescalation with the nearly unlimited risks of violent escalation, but states may take that risk. Although violent escalation is beyond the scope of this chapter, it does present a serious risk that those that would escalate in cyberspace cannot ignore.

Escalation Risks

Just as deterrence works only if the adversary believes it does, so too with escalation: The adversary's perception of red lines determines whether one's own cyberattacks are escalatory. The fact that adversaries determine what is escalatory sets the context for this chapter's question: What is the escalatory potential inherent in cyberattacks? We examine three contexts: precrisis preparations, operational cyberwar within local conflicts, and escalation beyond operational cyberwar.

Escalation Risks in Phase 0

A state that faces the prospect of kinetic conflict should anticipate being hit by cyberattacks. Yet, if it views the prospect of conflict as possible rather than inevitable, it faces a choice. Modulating its activities may avoid exciting the other side and contribute to a peaceful resolution, but it may also signal distaste for battle and leave vulnerabilities untended—both of which may encourage a determinedly hostile state.

Five activities may characterize phase 0 activities in cyberspace: (1) increasing defensive preparations, (2) demonstrating offensive capabilities, (3) accelerating cyberespionage (e.g., to find more vulnerabilities), (4) inserting implants and back doors (e.g., to facilitate attack), and (5) disrupting problematic communication outlets. Each one carries its own type of escalation risk.

Increasing cyberdefensive preparations should carry little escalation risk. Most such preparations are invisible to the adversary. They are generally not adversary-specific. Furthermore, they are also entirely legitimate. Nevertheless, benign outcomes are not guaranteed. Some preparations will be hard to hide (e.g., cutting users off from the Internet). Also, if the state bulwarking its defenses wishes to communicate as much in order to dampen an adversary's temptation to carry out a first strike, some preparations must perforce become visible. The adversary can concede their legitimate nature and think nothing more of the attempt. But adversaries are constantly assessing the intentions of their rivals and may conclude that defensive preparations are being made in order that offensive cyberattacks later be carried out with impunity (as discussed in Chapter Six). A great deal depends on what the adversary takes to be an indication and what it takes to be a warning.

Demonstrating offensive capabilities, by contrast, is both visible and invisible if successful. It may be regarded as hostile, particularly when carried out during a crisis. It is definitely a warning to adversaries not to start trouble, but it may also convince adversaries that trouble is coming. A lot may depend on whether the state that is witnessing such demonstrations believes that it is being coerced to yield or settle. If asked to yield, it may bridle. If asked to settle, it may reason that demonstrating cyberattack capabilities may make a point at the cost of reducing its later effectiveness by hinting at the target's vulnerabilities. Such a conclusion would suggest that a shot across a bow is more of a reminder than a preattack maneuver. Again, a great deal depends on how the adversary thinks.

Accelerating cyberespionage should also be invisible, hence unproductive of trouble. Discovering the odd penetration is no proof that activity has accelerated because cyberespionage is always taking place, unless the discovered penetration affects systems previously thought off-limits to attack. Again, a lot depends on the things to which the adversary reacts.

Inserting implants follows the same logic: They should be invisible. Even if implants are found, they may arguably be prefatory to cyberespionage rather than cyberattack. Nevertheless, the adversary may find such implants to be akin to discovering mines in their waters: clearly hostile and putatively an act of war. Although earlier chapters cautioned that finding them ought not necessarily create a crisis, adversaries may not heed such cautions.[10]

Finally, using cyberattacks to disable contentious communication channels, such as web sites that incite to violence, may be a step in favor of crisis resolution or may be viewed as a violation of sovereignty.[11] The helpful conclusion requires that adversaries (1) feel that such web sites were themselves unhelpful but lacked the skills or the political cover to disable such sites themselves and (2) are more likely to let their private relief rather than the public posturing guide their actions.

Escalation Risks for Contained Local Conflicts

In theory, operational cyberwar—carrying out cyberattacks on targets that are considered legitimate war targets—should not be considered escalatory. It is just another way to accomplish the same end, and with fewer lives at risk. But sometimes, an act is judged escalatory based not on what it does but how it does it (e.g., taking out a bunker with chemical weapons is considered more heinous than doing the same job with

---

[10] The discovery of one piece of malware tends to increase the odds of finding others of both the same type and different types. The first malware suggests the possibility of a systematic campaign, which, if nothing else, favors intensifying search efforts; greater search tends to lead to more finds. In some cases, the signature of the discovered malware (or the communications to the C2 server) may help identify subsequent copies and even derivatives (much as the discovery of Stuxnet may have somewhat hastened the discovery of Duqu and Flame). Unfortunately for crisis management, it may be hard for the public to distinguish a cascade of discoveries bunched closely in time from a cascade of attacks that are similarly bunched. The actual attacks may have, in fact, been emplaced over a far longer period in the past.

[11] If the affected web site is in a third country, legalities and the reaction of the latter may have to be taken into account.

high explosives).[12] The Japanese considered the first use of firebombing (March 1945) to be escalatory even though the attack on Dresden, Germany, had already taken place. The use of cruise missiles in Bosnia (1995) was considered escalatory.[13] Although it is unclear whether such sentiments were anything more than sentiments (because neither target could escalate in response), the broader point stands.

If opponents believe that cyberweapons have mysterious effects, their use will be seen as escalatory even though, measured in terms of actual effects, they should not be. Adversaries may also convince themselves that, although the cyberattacks per se were in bounds, their use against military targets portends their use against civilian targets because the latter can be surreptitiously attacked via cyberspace even if kinetic attacks on them would be universally considered off-limits. Again, it depends on what adversaries think.

Escalation Risks for Uncontained Conflicts

Cyberescalation beyond the immediate local conflict can go down one of several paths,[14] and each path carries its own escalation risk.

One path is to attack systems with effects beyond the conflict zone. Thus, attacks on a system that supports local combat operations may disable the adversary's ability to carry out other operations. Such systems could physically sit in the theater or, alternatively, out of the theater; in cyberspace, physical location is almost an afterthought. Although legitimate targets of war and cyberattacks on them ought not be considered escalatory, the adversary's perspectives are what matter.

Another path is to attack systems that have civilian uses. Some of these may be systems that control homeland assets that are used to support a war (e.g., a cyberattack on the management of a military port in the homeland). Further along the path is an attack on dual-use facili-

---

[12] Using means rather than ends as the measuring rod of escalation downplays the possibility that means may be shifted, not to gain an advantage but because prior means have been rendered unavailable. Cyberattacks, for instance, may be used as an attempt to replace effects that electronic warfare previously offered.

[13] Morgan et al., 2008.

[14] A similar point is made in Kahn, 1965, p. 5.

ties (e.g., that port supported both commercial shipping and military logistics). Even further along the path is an attack on a primarily civilian activity: a power plant that supplies a city but also an integrated air defense system. A larger step by way of escalation is to attack a facility *with the intent* of persuading civilians to pressure their government into suing for peace. Such attacks are more likely than the purely military attacks to be perceived as escalation.[15] How the other side creates narratives around such attacks may determine what kind of response may be forthcoming. One approach is righteous wrath: The cyberattacker has escalated a local conflict into a global conflict, and all restraints are off. Another would use the attack on the homeland to mobilize its population to support the remote conflict but confine the response to the theater. Or the adversary, unwilling to escalate a local into a global conflict, can just shrug the attack off.

There are escalation steps even within the category of coercive attacks. Attacks on infrastructure are bad, but attacks that disable or disrupt safety systems (e.g., air traffic control) are worse, and those whose sole purpose is to create civilian casualties (e.g., hospital medication monitors) are worst. The closer cyberattacks get to civilians, the more likely they are to violate the laws of armed conflict and UN treaties. Finally, strategic attacks imply that states *can* be coerced, which is insulting and not just injurious (whereas it is no insult if other states try to disarm a state).

The third path entails attacks on systems that portend wider conflict (e.g., on strategic warning systems or, more broadly, corruption attacks that may make the target worry about the quality of its over-

---

[15] Would an attack on an information system, such as a cloud host, situated in the territory of an innocent third party but critical to the conduct of the adversary's campaign be considered out of bounds? Perhaps that question is premature. First, militaries are more reluctant than commercial enterprises to entrust their critical information to neutral third parties even if their information is encrypted. Second, only some of the ways of attacking such information systems are attacks on someone else's "territory": Client-side corruption probably would not count, and it is unclear whether exploiting a flaw in the server's software to corrupt data content would count either; conversely, disabling a particular server might raise third-country issues especially if the server has other customers. Might matters be modulated if the third country were told of the risks assumed by its hosting databases that support a third country's wars?

all C2 over both fighters and weapons). Similarly, crippling systems that hamper the target state's ability to maintain its hold on power may be misinterpreted as prefatory to a regime-change campaign. The same holds for disruptive but especially corrupting attacks on state-friendly media and internal security systems. If the adversary is nervous enough about internal stability, then a cyberattack on the capability of its domestic security forces may trigger a panicked and potential escalatory response (unless such attacks persuade the adversary to back off and conclude that bigger stakes than information security are on the table). Similarly, something like the (so-called) Great Firewall of China would be off-limits, despite how richly apropos a target it may appear. A related set of attacks to avoid is one that undermines the basic trust that citizens have in their government and comparable institutions (e.g., corruption attacks on the financial system). Systems behind which the adversary has put public prestige—perhaps because they allow it to fulfill an important promise or because they have been touted as secure—may also force the attacker to escalate.

The effect that strategic cyberwarfare can have on the narrative of conflict also has to be considered. A state whose conflict goals are local and definite may unwittingly create another narrative by escalating into the other side's homeland. It may aver that the purpose of such attacks was operational in that the target systems directly supported the adversary's war operations, or coercive in that it expected the population to demand that the local conflict be brought to an end. The besieged state may justifiably conclude that the purpose of these attacks was regime change and react as if the stakes had changed. It might work: Attacks on Belgrade and on facilities owned by friends of Milošević may have convinced the regime that losing Kosovo was better than losing everything,[16] but the risks of a response should not be overlooked.

---

[16] Stephen T. Hosmer, *The Conflict Over Kosovo: Why Milosevic Decided to Settle When He Did*, Santa Monica, Calif.: RAND Corporation, MR-1351-AF, 2001.

Managing Proxy Cyberattacks

Proxy cyberattacks may well be a feature of future wars if and when many states acquire the requisite offensive cybercapability and their targets acquire systems that are simultaneously important to warfighting and vulnerable to attack. Third parties may have all manner of reasons to jump in. They may wish to weaken one side or another's ability to carry out military operations. Perhaps, they would like to see the conflicts of others grow harder to withdraw from thereby letting such third parties wreak mischief in other neighborhoods with greater confidence they will not be interfered with. Such attacks may also be carried out as a live-fire training exercise or as active pinging—a way to collect intelligence that passive methods cannot offer. The attractions of third-party meddling are enhanced by the reduced likelihood of getting caught: Not only are multiple parties wreaking mischief at the same time, but each combatant's tendency would be to blame cyberattacks on its battlefield foes rather than on third parties.

To the extent that proxy cyberattacks matter, each party to a conflict may have to think about how to suppress such attacks without creating new escalation challenges. In this section, we examine two scenarios: (1) when third parties are covert and (2) when their participation is overt.

What Hidden Combatants Imply for Horizontal Escalation

A two-party conflict may easily become a multiparty free-for-all in cyberspace, making attribution more difficult and creating difficult decisions about how to recognize and respond to third-party attackers. To illustrate as much, consider a cybercrisis between the United States and Iran that arises from a politico-military crisis.

So far, the contest seems simple: the United States versus Iran, with the prospect that each will carry out cyberattacks on the other. More to the point, the first suspect in any attack on U.S. forces will be Iran and vice versa. Assume, for the sake of discussion, that the United States has self-imposed limits on its own cyberattacks (e.g., it will not attack civilian targets unless necessary to hinder Iranian military capabilities or operations).

Iran, in this scenario, however, may well have multiple targets for its cyberwarriors. They include the U.S. military and anything that can annoy the United States (unless they think that an enraged United States is a more dangerous foe). But would Iran stop there? For historical reasons, the Iranians tend to blame the United Kingdom more than a neutral reading of Iran's circumstances would warrant: Such attacks may be meant as punishment for real or imagined offenses since, but may also be meant to discourage possible UK involvement. Other potential targets include Sunni Arab states that have made no secret of their fear of Iran (and that may be inclined to help U.S. kinetic and cyberforces). If Iran follows Saddam Hussein's logic from the first Gulf War, it may eye Israel as a target as well as a way of goading Israel into doing something that may alienate its Sunni Arab foes.

Conversely, it is by no means obvious that those Iran would target are waiting patiently to be attacked before they respond. Iran's foes may figure that a cyberattack on Iran would help U.S. efforts. If the United States has, in their view, unwisely retrained its own operations, it may hope to goad Iran into striking nonmilitary targets of the United States by striking corresponding targets within Iran, thereby deepening the U.S. commitment.

Such third parties would be a minor problem compared with what would arise should a seriously competent cyberpower (e.g., Russia or China) get into the fray. Cyberspace permits such powers to curry favor with one side without necessarily making the other side an enemy—something that would be very difficult for combatants in the physical world, where attribution is more, albeit not perfectly, obvious (in that sense, carrying out cyberattacks has many of the same attributes as lending support by providing intelligence). Such third parties may also have a stake in starting or, conversely, halting a crisis: If the crisis turns into conflict, they have a stake in the outcome. A last motivation for outside powers is to find out where the U.S. military is vulnerable to a disruptive attack, as well as how the U.S. military would respond to an attack. A grateful Iran would be more than willing to supply them intelligence on U.S. forces of the sort that could be gained only by being in hostile contact with them. Iran can also lend them platforms from which to test attacks that require being within range to U.S. radio-frequency (RF) networks. If there are two such powers, Iran could play one off against the other. Normally, this interest could not be pursued, given the consequences of getting caught, but, if one combatant will be predisposed to blame its adversary rather than a third party for any mischief in cyberspace, it may figure that the risks are lower (conversely, the victim may make a point of warning third parties away from interference by threatening harsher reprisals and an itchier trigger finger precisely because third parties create such troubling issues).

With these dramatis personae at play, how can the United States navigate in these treacherous waters without unnecessarily broadening its conflict? A cavalcade of cyberattacks, failures, misread results, collateral damage, cascading effects, narratives of power, accusations, overconfident attempts at attribution, retaliation based on such attribution, and counterretaliation are all possibilities.

What would the United States do with knowledge that Iran is getting help? Perhaps it would be in the U.S. interest to "discover" that Iran had carried out the more-sophisticated attacks if it solidifies domestic support for military operations. It may also be easier to convince everyone to take cyberdefense more seriously if they believe that a middling power, such as Iran, could carry out sophisticated cyberattacks.

True, such an approach would hardly discourage major cyberpowers. Yet, how badly should the United States want to discourage them? Having them attack U.S. forces throws a spotlight on what they can do; there is intelligence to be mined there. Unfortunately, as noted, it also gives *them* a fairly good hint about what U.S. forces can do—and so there is intelligence for *them* to mine there. Who learns more quickly? Can the United States usefully deceive others about its capabilities better than they can deceive the United States about theirs?

Otherwise, how could third parties be persuaded to stop? First, they would have to be convinced that the United States knows they are up to no good rather than believe that the United States is casting about for someone (other than Iran) to blame because the going is rougher than expected. Complaints need to be credible. Second, they would have to believe that the United States could put sufficient leverage on them, either through sub-rosa channels or by taking the chance of going public and doing something before the entire world. If the United States does go public, will third parties deny their participation and argue that the United States is just whining? If their denials are absent or at least insincere, will they back down or conclude that, having been so accused, in for a dime, in for a dollar? If the latter, would they support Iran more overtly—say, with intelligence or equipment—thereby complicating U.S. efforts? In today's environment, in which Iran is the most powerful country that does *not* value stable relations with the United States, denial seems the more likely, unless the United States really pushes the matter. Either way, the U.S. gains from acting on its knowledge may be mixed.

Incidentally, this scenario should illustrate why horizontal escalation, the successive entry of the uninvolved into a war on one or both sides (or how World War I started), is of lesser concern with wars in cyberspace. It is difficult to know who is *not* a combatant in cyberspace at any point in time. Furthermore, the entry of others may not matter nearly as much as it does in conventional conflict, in which numbers matter: One state that joins its forces with another to fight as one can tip the battle. In cyberspace, arithmetic superiority does not mean the same. True, two entities combining their search for vulnerabilities in the same target are likely to be more rather than less efficient, but only if they coordinate their efforts correctly.[17] The likelihood that such cyberwar entities work in nonmutual compartments suggests that this is less likely. Furthermore, given the likelihood that the roster of unexploited and accessible vulnerabilities in the adversary get slimmer after the initial cyberattacks, synergy requires that the two partners be working together *well before* conflict has started, which, by definition, is not escalation.

---

[17] Adding the forces of one to the search agenda for the other, conversely, may not be as efficient as having each partner pursue its own approach separately, *if* a failure in imagination rather than a shortfall of effort better explains why attempts to penetrate an adversary's system falls short.

Managing Overt Proxy Conflict

Proxy war may also take place when a state with sophisticated cyber-operators openly supports one side in a local war. Even if outsiders play by Las Vegas rules (what takes place in-theater stays in-theater), information systems span the world. The mischief perpetrated from outside the theater can affect systems in theater and vice versa. In physical combat—using the Korean and Vietnam wars as examples—the bounds between allowable and proscribed targets were mostly observed. Chinese forces were fair game for U.S. forces below but not above the Yalu River. Russians avoided the Korean theater except for (possible) air combat. U.S. forces were not attacked out of theater. During the First Indochina War, the United States was liberal in sending France supplies, but not people. In the Vietnam War, similar rules applied: In theory, Russian and Chinese "advisers" to North Vietnamese forces manning Russian or Chinese equipment, mostly SAMs, were not explicitly off-limits. Yet, some U.S. policymakers worried about unintentionally killing them (while others were disappointed that they escaped harm).

Are Las Vegas rules possible? Will cyberwar assistance be considered akin to supplies or forces? The fact that cyberwar involves people says forces, but the immunity of cyberwarriors sitting out of theater makes it look more like supplies. Local hackers may be trained on and supplied with exploit tools, information on vulnerabilities, and intelligence on targets. After all that, figuratively pulling the trigger may add very little to culpability.

The links between a local combatant's and its great power friend's systems may color whether friends of each side come to blows. Can systems operated by the local combatant be attacked without interfering with systems of its great power friends? Are the systems the friend brings into theater densely connected to its own global systems? If one side's friend harms the in-theater systems of the other side's friend, would the latter want to make an issue of it? Can the attacker's friend argue local military necessity? Can the target's friend retort that the attack was meant to harm it directly and not influence the local fight? Physical boundaries of the sort that help distinguish acceptable from unacceptable behavior are not as reliable a guide in cyberspace, so the usual firebreaks do not exist. One can imagine a continually escalating confrontation that, at some point, requires either negotiations of some sort to establish a new and less obvious firebreak or, failing that, calls for one or the other party to back down unilaterally, lest general war in cyberspace ensue.

So what norms should apply? In some cases, physical boundaries may, for lack of a better alternative, stand in for cyberboundaries. Systems that sit outside the war zone are off-limits to a cyberattack even if they help the local combatant fight, just as supplies warrant a similar status. However, the same would not apply to in-theater portals to such a system. Hence the question: How much should an attacker be expected to know about how local systems and access points are connected to global systems of the great power friend?

Potential asymmetries plague the application of any such norms. If, on one side, local combatants and its global friend kept a good wall between their systems, but the other side does not, then attacking the one side's local systems would carry less risk of escalation than attacking the other side's local systems. Why should the latter get a free pass just because of its architecture? Such asymmetries are compounded by ambiguities in cyberspace. If the citizens of one side's friend depend on capabilities that go haywire if those of its local combatant ally are hacked (such systems could easily sit in third countries), and the other side attacks and claims that its attacks were legitimate, will the other side be seen as credible or as opportunistic?

Avoiding escalation in such scenarios might require such great powers to carefully separate their global systems from those sent to theater and require attackers to exercise great caution to ensure that their cyberattacks have precise effects—never easy, even under the best of circumstances. But it would not hurt for either side to realize that accidents happen, especially in war zones.

The Difficulties of Tit-for-Tat Management

In 1980, after running a set of extended prisoner's dilemma contests, Robert Axelrod concluded that a tit-for-tat strategy was the optimal one.[18] Tit-for-tat strategy is simple: Do not start a fight; if hit, hit back on the next turn; if not hit on a turn, do not hit back on the next turn. The strategy's extension to escalation is straightforward. Not for nothing do states respond to escalation with escalation of their own in the justified belief that such a strategy is best suited to ensure that no one escalates. Hence, intrawar deterrence (the threat of counterescalation as a way of inhibiting the escalation of combatants).[19]

Yet, the extension of such a strategy to cyberspace is problematic. The case for tit-for-tat strategy assumes that intent equals effects equals perceptions. But cyberspace is sufficiently noisy that tit-for-tat strategies may have harmful effects. The problems of intrawar deterrence may be as daunting as the problems of deterrence overall.

The Importance of Preplanning

Cyberattacks, particularly against hard targets, require considerable scoping of the target. Those who wrote the Stuxnet worm, for instance, took many months understanding the relationship between the Siemens programmable logic chip for which the worm was written and the Iranian centrifuge plant whose operations it was trying to hinder. Planning for conventional strikes is more straightforward and typically much quicker, particularly if there are no worries about getting the delivery vehicle home safely.

The need for prewar planning carries implications for escalation management. If not done, the list of targets that can be struck immediately will be correspondingly reduced. Most of the easy targets will be those that are easy because they are not important, hence not well defended. However, some of the easy targets may be those that were

---

[18] The problem and the strategy, developed by Anatol Rapaport, are discussed in Robert Axelrod, *The Evolution of Cooperation*, New York: Basic Books, 1984. The term *prisoner's dilemma* describes a situation in which each of two players (prisoners) must choose whether to compete with (by ratting on) or cooperate with (by staying silent about) the other. Each player's individual advantage lies with competing with the other (whether or not the other player competes or cooperates), but both would be better off if they both cooperated.

[19] Intrawar deterrence consists of threats against acknowledged adversaries as a way of limiting the depth, breadth, or frequency of their attacks; interwar deterrence is meant against those that have yet to attack.

not particularly well guarded because their owners did not conceive that anyone would profit from attacking them. Thus, hospitals tend not to be the most security-conscious institutions, compared to say, banks.

If commanders want to escalate and have not prepared the cyber-battlefield, their options are limited, leaving mostly targets whose disruption or corruption would have low and hence unimpressive impacts or those that have high impacts by virtue of their shock value. Unfortunately, shock value is not conducive to escalation management.

Thus, it helps for a state to think through its possible target set in advance.[20] It may decide to put certain targets off-limits and therefore not scope them, but it cannot change its mind instantly.

As a corollary, a cyberattack that fails to elicit a retaliatory response may be interpreted as one that did not cross the other side's red line. The truth may be that the victimized state, surprised to be attacked in that way, had simply not developed a capability to respond in kind.

Disjunctions Among Effort, Effect, and Perception

A tit-for-tat strategy that works well in a quiet environment may not work so well in a noisy one. An important problem arises from the potential discordance among intentions, effects, perceptions, and announcements. As noted, predicting battle damage is extremely difficult. Facing that problem, those that would escalate may try a shotgun approach, hoping that something will break. By doing so, they effectively renounce any precision in escalation management. They also give up trying to make a point by attacking a particularly symbolic target and, instead, widen their target set and flaunt whatever works. Although the success of the Stuxnet worm suggests that individual targeting is possible, the attackers were not aiming for a precisely calibrated effect: The more damage, the better. Furthermore, the preparation for the attack was believed to have been years during which there

---

[20] Note that intelligence preparation of the cyberbattlefield, as it were, may differ sharply from everyday CNE. The former is concerned with understanding the target system well enough to understand what commands may make it act in a disruptive, destructive, or corrupted manner. It focuses on the instruction architecture of the target system. The latter tends to be a massive file-extraction exercise. It focuses on the content architecture of the target system.

was no reason for Natanz to suddenly increase its cybersecurity. By contrast, such preparation in the context of a war either presumes a very short war or risks stumbling when the security status of the targeted system shifts from a peacetime to a wartime mode.

The potential mismatch between effects and perceptions is another part of the same coin. The direct effects of a cyberattack may be obvious: The lights go out, for example. But, if the cyberattack is sufficiently complex, spreads very widely, or involves corrupted data (which, at first, appears valid), the true damage may be obscured even to the target. But perceptions rather than effects are the things to which the target state would react.

Last is the mismatch between perceptions and announcements whenever the damage is less than public. Obvious damage (such as the lights going out) is hard to misrepresent, particularly in our transparent times (once the damage is correctly characterized). But damage may not always be so obvious, especially if the system that is damaged does not have enough of a performance record to establish what normal operations look like. As noted, Iran's line on Stuxnet continued to evolve. Although announcements would seem secondary to perceptions, they may be the only information that third-party observers, the street, and even those outside the immediate circle of power will get.

Overall, the gearing between intent and consequence is multijointed and loose. Thus, a state may attempt escalation and (1) succeed, (2) fail but in such a way as to make no one the wiser, or (3) fail in ways that make it obvious that something was attempted but did not work. The latter simultaneously demonstrates malice and incompetence and may lead to overreaction as a way for the attacking state to regain the narrative. Alternatively, a state may just not respond when it could have, and something fails mysteriously anyway. It could be an accident, a rogue operative, a third-party state, or simply the inability of the target state to distinguish occasional failure from normal operations. So the target responds as if escalation had really taken place.

Finally, in cyberspace, the intent to react to escalation cannot necessarily be demonstrated as such. In the Vietnam War, escalation meant adding troops: easy to announce and verify. In cyberspace, neither the quality nor the number of the troops is obvious or can be reliably monitored; indeed, these are usually highly secret. If there really is *any* ongoing conflict, there is no reason for a state *not* to assign all of its cyberattackers to the effort. Unlike, say, soldiers or sailors, they do not have to be deployed around the world in case another war breaks out, and it is not as if they cost more deployed than standing around.[21] The effects of making a greater effort may be long in coming; finding vulnerabilities is more like an investment, in which throwing more people at finding vulnerabilities produces more vulnerabilities—if they exist at all—only after a certain amount of time.[22] Furthermore, many of the best hacks are unnoticed by their victims until inexplicable failures start to mount. Only outputs count.

Inadvertent Escalation

A tit-for-tat strategy may also lead to unintended consequences, particularly if the red lines on each side are unannounced or, if announced, not compatible.

Figure 4.2 illustrates what may occur in a local war in which both parties have thresholds but define them differently. The attacker, in this example, the United States, starts by hacking into the target's afloat naval supply facility database in order to scramble its contents. The target takes this as a cyberattack on military support and responds by hacking into the software system that controls Guam's port, to do likewise. The United States takes this to be an attack on the homeland (Guam being a U.S. territory), and it hacks into the software that controls port operations on the target's mainland. The target takes this as an attack on its civilian infrastructure. And so on.

All this escalation takes place even though neither side, at any time, believes that it is escalating. Each side is carrying out operations inside the boundaries within which the other side is already working. Yet, between the two, escalation happens. Although similar issues

---

[21] The same claim cannot be made for cyberespionage, in which one hesitates to pull cyberwarriors from one country of interest, such as China, just because they may be useful to deal with a conflict elsewhere. But cyberattackers have no alternative cyberattack activity in peacetime.

[22] Stuxnet was estimated to have a gestation of a year, give or take a factor or two, and that may have been *after* the necessary zero-day attacks were discovered.

Figure 4.2
An Inadvertent Path to Mutual Escalation

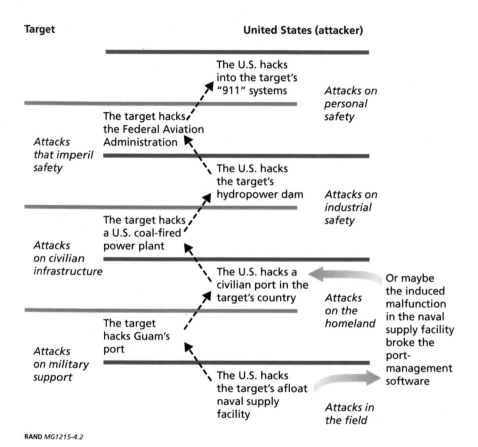

RAND MG1215-4.2

bedevil escalation management in the kinetic world, the United States has no reasonable fear of having its homeland touched by another state in the physical world.[23] No such guarantees exist in cyberspace.

Alas, asymmetries between opponents will complicate tacit agreements on what to leave intact in the cyberworld, just as they do in the physical world. A local conflict between the United States and China over Taiwan will take place much closer to China: Agreeing

---

[23] Terrorism constitutes an exception, but one that is limited by virtue of the kind of weapons that can be brought into the United States and close to the target without being detected.

that homeland ports are off-limits favors China because the gains to it from attacking embarking ports in, say, California are likely to be quite diffuse given the long steaming times. The reverse favors the United States. One country may use coal to generate its electricity; the other, hydropower. A policy that has each side refrain, for safety reasons, from interfering with dam controls unfairly penalizes the coal-using state; only its electrical generating capacity remains at risk. States that have built dedicated communication lines for defense are disadvantaged against states that must depend on dual-use infrastructures if both agree not to target dual-use nodes routers and switches. States that feed intelligence to "patriotic" hackers to carry out cyberattacks are at an advantage over those who depend on their own employees if the onus against cyberattacks is levied only against warfighters acting under state command.

Without announced red lines, states have to calculate how far they can go without touching the other side's nerves—and the extent to which adversaries will game such calculations. Similar issues associated with physical attacks can be dealt with through geographical limitations on combat: e.g., Northern Watch operations (circa 1993) did not extend below the 36th parallel. Boundaries in cyberspace are harder to define and confine. A reported U.S. strike on a jihadist web site supposedly took out 300 servers around the world.[24] Indeed, information system support for combat operations need not be anywhere near the conflict, RF bandwidth permitting; they are more survivable if they are not. So, a subtle adversary may deliberately outsource such processing to server clouds located in third-party countries. Thus, the useful boundaries have to be logical rather than physical ones. Unfortunately, as Schelling points out, such boundaries will limit the activities of both sides only if they are negotiated or obvious (e.g., stopping at the river's edge).[25] Otherwise, they seem arbitrary and meaningless, and therefore not credible guides to the other side's red lines; or, alternatively, concocted to favor the side that advocates them. The nuclear threshold was

---

[24] Ellen Nakashima, "Dismantling of Saudi-CIA Web Site Illustrates Need for Clearer Cyberwar Policies," *Washington Post*, March 19, 2010, p. A1.

[25] His theory of the focal point was developed in Schelling, 1960, pp. 53–80.

one such boundary. The distinction between fatal and nonfatal cyber-attacks may be another. Avoiding the strategic path is a little trickier because a cyberattack can run this escalation path without the attacker and, for a while, even the target, realizing as much. Although the dual-use nature of some command, control, communications, computers, intelligence, surveillance, and reconnaissance systems may present similar difficulties for physical escalation, such problems are trickier in cyberspace to the extent that the virtual connections between systems are less visible. Thus, it is difficult to ascertain whether a strategic system was or was not depending on some capability or utility that was knocked out by a cyberattack meant to cripple a conventional capability. Indeed, if the wiring diagram between systems is sufficiently complicated, the target may not know that its strategic systems have been crippled until afterward.[26]

Finally, because the collateral effects of cyberwar are poorly understood, escalation-management strategies have to reflect the possibility of accidents. As shown on the right of Figure 4.2, the attack on the target's afloat naval supply facility may corrupt information, thus breaking the port-management software in that country (how was the United States to know that the target's port-management software did not do a sanity check on the information coming in from its ships?). Such accidents give further impetus to escalation in an environment in which both sides cannot bear escalation without matching it. Incidentally, no state should count on being able to argue that some effect was an accident, that it will not be repeated, and that accidents do not justify counterescalation by the other side. States rarely apologize even

---

[26] The strategic question of whether a state in a nonnuclear confrontation should raise a shadow over nuclear systems as part of its brinkmanship strategy is a separate issue not mooted here. If a state concludes against such a strategy, its policy on the use of cyber-weapons should conform by staying as far away from the other side's nuclear C2 as it can (short of clear evidence that strategic weapons are about to fly or the threat to release them has already been made). Once a state thinks that its C2 is weak, it starts worrying about whether it has to use nuclear weapons while it still has control over them (whether such logic would apply if it fears that its systems might already be disrupted beforehand is a different issue). Similarly, if it starts to distrust its strategic surveillance, it may allow itself to make launch decisions based on less reliable but more trustworthy (for their not having been attacked) systems.

when wrong, and victimized states rarely settle for mere apology; reparations *during* wartime are even less common.[27] More typically, once a breach has been made, it tends to be exploited with vigor rather than backed away from.[28]

Escalation into Kinetic Warfare

Under what circumstances can an attack limited to cyberspace or a conflict carried on by both sides only in cyberspace escalate into kinetic warfare and therefore violence? Are the two realms considered distinct and therefore unrelated, or are they part of the same continuum of force? Iran did not respond to Stuxnet with violence against the United States or Israel (but nor did Syria, for that matter, respond with violence to Israel's destruction of a purported nuclear reaction in 2007 despite hints that Israel used cyberwar techniques to help with air attack).

Several considerations merit note.

First, signals could be indicative. The more that a state has declared that it would respond to a cyberattack (that crossed some threshold), the greater the loss in face if it does not. If the attacker has few assets at risk from cyberwar (e.g., the Democratic People's Republic of Korea [DPRK]), the choice becomes one of either not responding meaningfully or responding with physical force. Likewise, the more that a state has rejected the idea of limiting a response to in kind, and the more it has embraced the concept of cross-domain deterrence (consider the smokestack reference earlier), the greater its odds of crossing from the virtual to the real world.

Second, hostile or at least bumptious action in certain domains seems to strike closer to home than do others. The United States and the Soviet Union had many incidents at sea, as noted earlier, and none

---

[27] The United States never apologized after downing an Iranian Airbus in 1988, although it did pay $62 million to settle subsequent claims eight years later. In 1904, the Imperial Russian fleet, thinking that it saw Japanese warships, attacked British fishermen and almost precipitated a war with England. See Gavin Weightman, *Industrial Revolutionaries: The Making of the Modern World 1776–1914*, London: Grove Atlantic, 2009, pp. 342–345.

[28] Kahn, 1965, p. 127.

of them escalated into actual war. The United States did not go to war when the DPRK captured the USS *Pueblo* in 1968 (nor break diplomatic relations with Israel over the sinking of the USS *Liberty* in 1967). Similarly, both sides ran active espionage operations against one another, and, with the possible exception of the furor associated with the Soviet downing of a U-2 aircraft, none of them seriously rippled the surface. This pattern has continued with espionage between Israel and its foes. Supposedly, U.S. and Soviet aircraft engaged one another during the Korea War without creating a broader crisis. By contrast, incidents involving Army soldiers (such as the death of MAJ Arthur D. Nicholson Jr. by East Germany in 1985, or the axe murder of 1LT Mark Barrett by North Koreans in 1976) seem to have had greater echoes. Would a cyberattack on the homeland be considered akin to a naval or intelligence incident and thus handled within its own channels? Or would it be considered akin to an army or homeland incident and thus lead to crisis and perhaps the use of force?

Third, the decision to use force—which is, in many cases, tantamount to starting a war—involves answering a set of questions, many of which have nothing to do with the incident that precipitated it. A rational state would ask itself, what would be gained by going to war? At what price? With what risk? But states, except for the most-obvious aggressors (e.g., Nazi Germany), often tell themselves that they are going to war because they have no choice other than to do so. That is, a world in which they do not go to war would be intolerable. Or the decision to refrain from war would only postpone conflict, not eliminate its possibility; when war came, outcomes would be worse, perhaps catastrophic.[29] Hence the question, what about a cyberattack would convince a state that it had no choice but to go to war? Clearly, the prospect of further cyberattacks would have to be considered intolerable. But the rationale to "take arms against a sea of troubles, and by opposing end them" presupposes that the use of force can end the pros-

---

[29] Examples may include a Wilhelmine Germany facing a steadily strengthening Russia and fearing encirclement, a Japan facing an economically devastating cutoff of raw materials, or an Iraq whose ability to pay war debts was being seriously crimped by Kuwaiti stubbornness about oil markets.

pect of cyberattacks. But can they? Given the difficulty of disarming hackers, such a prospect would appear to be dim. If the hackers capable of causing so much trouble emigrated, even occupation of their countries would not necessarily end their capabilities (although it would stoke revanchist motivations). That leaves, as a rationale for the use of force, the prospect of deterrence. A state punished severely enough for having launched cyberattacks against another might hesitate before doing it again; states that are watching may feel similarly disinclined. But this logic presumes that the state in question, as well as onlookers, convinces itself that it was the cyberattack that led to the use of force.

Escalation into Economic Warfare

Another source of crisis exacerbation is the tendency for a trade war to overtake and become proxy for a budding cyberwar.

Indeed, it is hard to imagine any serious strategic cyberwar between two trade-linked states that does *not* become a trade war, and part of the art of managing a cybercrisis with a trading state is how to manage such fallout. This cuts two ways. A state can work to ensure that little of the cyberwar spills into the trading arena. Or it can use the threat of a trade war, coupled with the credible ability to wage one, to terminate a nascent cyberwar.

To illustrate, take the conflict scenario described in Chapter Six of *Cyber War*.[30] China starts by claiming all the South China Sea. The United States says no and conducts exercises with some newfound Asian friends. The United States leads the attack in cyberspace, first by sending China a warning in the form of an image of a sinking ship emailed from within China's supposedly closed military network, and then by turning off the power around the ports from which a potential Chinese amphibious invasion of disputed islands is being assembled—which unfortunately blacks out the entire province of Guangdong. This China considers escalatory. China retaliates in kind—and also

---

[30] Richard A. Clarke and Robert K. Knake, *Cyber War: The Next Threat to National Security and What to Do About It*, New York: Ecco, 2010, pp. 179–218.

blacks out more of the West Coast than intended. Things go south quickly: Key financial databases are scrambled, and the control computers for the major U.S. railroads and airlines go down. So the United States ups the ante, only to discover that China has disconnected itself from the Internet, thus blocking the most obvious route into China's cyberspace. It also phased down power interconnects among its regional power grids, thus limiting the possibility of cascading failures. Finally, China placed its railroads under manual control. In the end, the United States decides that it has less stomach for cyberconflict than the Chinese appear to and essentially throws in the towel, but not without first sending more carriers into the area.

Clarke's *Cyber War* scenario is decided by each side's susceptibility to a cyberwar, but the contest ends quickly before each side's susceptibility to a trade war is fully tested. Granted, a weekend (the interval over which the entire conflict takes place) hardly provides much time for a trade war. Even so, the economic ramifications of what was described in the scenario merit contemplation. China's willingness to cut itself from the Internet is likely to affect China's ability to export. China's export sector, much of which is products made to order for large customers, depends on large data flows of product specifications from U.S. manufacturers and on sales from U.S. marketers. The United States exports a lot less than it imports from China, and a large share of its exports are long-production items, such as aircraft, that, by virtue of long production runs, may be less sensitive than short-production items to temporary information outages. The asymmetry favors the United States. If the disruption lasts more than a few weeks, Western investors in China stand to lose a great deal of money. China's attraction as a manufacturing base would dip relative to other low-cost producers elsewhere in Asia and Latin America. China's physical investments in the West, although growing, are far smaller than the West's investments there.[31] A large share of China's investments outside China is in

---

[31] Chinese investments in the West have tended to be portfolio investments, such as stocks, bonds, and other financial instruments; until 2009, China's direct investments in the United States averaged $500 million per year or less, compared with several billion dollars per year coming from the United States, according to statistics from the U.S.-China Business Coun-

commodity extraction, in which the questions, such as the protection of intellectual property in cyberspace, are nugatory.

Even today's cyberespionage can be economically costly for China; the 2010 Google incident (in which the company's systems were penetrated and source code stolen) has reinforced the wariness that many Western corporations have felt at locating too much intellectual property where it can be stolen, and China cannot have been pleased when GE's president criticized China's challenging business conditions.[32]

Were China's cyberoffensive to include supply-chain attacks,[33] the damage to the United States may be sharper, depending on how many zombie components exist in U.S. systems and whether they can be accessed and activated by hackers when needed.[34] A scenario of a supply-chain attack *outside the context of war* is implausible largely because many zombie components can be replaced over time: admittedly, months and perhaps years compared with the hours and days associated with restoring penetrated systems. But, again, there would be a severe risk to China's export base—particularly its economic export base—that would follow the revelation of a deliberate supply-chain attack. The echoes may well last a generation.[35]

---

cil. See Thilo Hanemann, "Chinese FDI in the United States: Q4 2011 Update," Rhodium Group, April 4, 2012.

[32] Heidi N. Moore, "GE's Jeff Immelt Says It Out Loud About China," *CNNMoney*, July 2, 2010.

[33] Which, admittedly, the Chinese may have more grounds to be afraid of than the United States would, given the U.S. dominance in software.

[34] A zombie computer is a user computer that a hacker can also control.

[35] In 2010, following a row with Japan over disputed islands, the supply of rare-earth minerals from China was suddenly tightened. Because rare-earth minerals are predominantly used in the electronic sector, this may have been an attempt to pressure one of Japan's leading export industries. Rare-earth minerals, name aside, however, are not really rare. The United States used to mine them in the Mojave Desert and could resurrect such a capability if customers started to get nervous enough to pay a premium for alternative supplies. This incident raises questions of what trade-offs China is willing to make between fostering a reputation as a reliable supplier and using its manufacturing position to pursue national security goals (Keith Bradsher, "Amid Tension, China Blocks Vital Exports to Japan," *New York Times*, September 22, 2010b).

All this, incidentally, may take place without U.S. policy pushing a trade war, which would violate many trade agreements unless open hostilities were going on. It suffices that the disruption through which China is willing to put its own industry in order to make a political point shifts the calculus of thousands of independent decisionmakers outside China. Corporations may be reluctant to complain in public lest they alone face China's wrath, but there are many more-subtle ways of registering dissatisfaction, not least of which is by doing nothing. Suddenly, China notices that no one returns its calls anymore.

The decision to allow or even encourage a freelance response to a cyberattack has two sides. The argument for control is that it permits the United States, as a target, to manage the crisis through explicit or implicit negotiations. The argument against control is that an attacker is more likely to be deterred by the unpredictable reactions of thousands that cannot be individually coerced than by the well-considered actions of a state that can be. Individuals can be inhibited by the prospect that their country may suffer, but, unless they are worried about getting caught *and* the act is proscribed (which does not necessarily apply to, say, a refusal to invest in China or buy Chinese products),[36] they themselves are not at risk. The logic is similar for a state-encouraged response. States that can create sufficient doubt that they are behind the "people's" response may escape punishment for encouraging a vigilante response. That noted, this is a trick that is harder for a government operating in a transparent society to carry out.

A freelance cyberresponse may be more likely than a freelance trade war but less worrisome. States do not have a monopoly on clever hackers but, in most cases, cleverness alone does not suffice to carry out damaging cyberattacks; it takes intelligence on targets, notably on the processes that may go haywire if such information systems are attacked. It is one thing, for instance, to make a system stop working; such systems can often be repaired or their faults routed around in days. It is quite another to make it work in such a way as to mislead

---

[36] The larger the organization, the more likely it is to have a track record of investing in or buying from China and the more likely a sudden change in its investment and purchasing behavior is likely to be noticed.

decisionmaking, corrupt data irreparably, or interfere with some process control and wreak serious havoc. Even if they can produce one or two audacious attacks, clever hackers suddenly aroused to fury will generally not have such intelligence with which to work. Deep intelligence is the province of states.

In deciding whether to escalate from cyberwar to a trade war, several other factors enter the equation. Is the cost of a trade war low compared with whatever concessions are entailed in losing a cyberwar? Can a credible threat to do so convince the other side not to take advantage of its superior cyberwar capability? Will the other side back down first? How much damage would a trade war wreak on the world trade system? Would the ever-tightening chain of global sourcing make everyone, including noncombatant states, worse off? Will there be pressure to carry on from potential winners of a trade war, countries that want to sell to one side but no longer have to compete with imports from its rival? These are familiar questions to any strategist contemplating a contest in which two states can only hurt one another (as well as bystanders) and so the first one who cries "uncle" loses.

Sub-Rosa Escalation

Another escalation option that might communicate displeasure to the other side without necessarily provoking it to respond is to strike systems whose malfunctioning will not be public even if apparent to the state's leadership.[37] The only entities that will *supposedly* know about the attack are the attacker, the target, and those to which either side confesses. Such limitations are meant to ease the pressure on the target to respond by escalation because no one can lose face (before the whole world) by backing off or not appearing tough enough. Sub-rosa options are generally unavailable to attackers in the physical world. Alternatively, cyberwarriors on both sides may be overcome by their own cleverness and create or exacerbate a crisis they cannot manage in

---

[37] This section and the accompanying Appendix B expand material that appeared in Libicki, 2009, pp. 128–129.

carrying out attacks and cyberattacks about which they thought only they knew. Done right, therefore, sub-rosa responses are likely to be less destabilizing than overt attacks and responses; done wrong, perhaps not so much. Appendix B examines sub-rosa operations within a broader three-by-three matrix of overt, obvious, and covert cyberattacks and responses.

Sub-rosa cyberattacks can be quite tempting, particularly among those within covert ranks. No one has to produce evidence of attribution. There is also less pressure to reveal the particulars (methodologies and targets) of the original attacks. Thus, the victims can pretend that nothing happened if they believe that they have no good counter-escalation options or wish to contain the level of overall damage. Indeed, there are many reasons that carrying out covert operations in cyberspace is easier than in the physical world: e.g., fewer potential prisoners.

Unfortunately, what is most attractive to some becomes a weakness to others. Those who work in the highly classified arena can avoid the *public* oversight under which the more-overt parts of the national security community operate.[38] If the attacker wishes to justify its actions, it has more control over what evidence is collected and presented; it has less to fear from contradictory material provided by neutral or hostile parties. It avoids having to answer the question, if the evidence of who carried out the original attack will be unconvincing to others, how good can it really be? Members of the covert community, despite their personal probity and honesty, tend to operate in a sealed world. Mistakes can go uncorrected for longer than those made by overt operators. When actions are criticized, members of the covert community tend to circle the wagons. Even those who argue that members of *one's own* covert community are like everybody else, only in different professions, the same may not hold for members of *other states'* covert community, in which rule of law is generally and noticeably weaker.

The second problem with sub-rosa warfare is that each side's strategy is hostage to the discretion exercised by the other side, not to men-

---

[38] This is not to say they get less oversight, overall, but it is necessarily by those that have access to the same information compartments.

tion accident and error. Once revelations start, many parties will be embarrassed—not only the attackers on both sides but also the targets for allowing vulnerabilities to pervade their system and covering up after these vulnerabilities were exploited. Although a primary rationale for keeping matters covert is to facilitate later settlement, covert communities are not always motivated by the desire to reach accommodation with the other side. Covert communities, by their nature, distrust all other covert communities. So, each side has to weigh whether it is better off pulling back the shades on these sub-rosa exchanges or letting matters continue their subterranean course. The result may be a game of chicken. Each knows that revelation will make its side look bad not only to the public but perhaps also to its own masters, but each may hope that the *threat* of revelation may make the other side accede. Each side may therefore be in a position to concede things to hide its mutual activities in ways that might be impossible were its "negotiations" subject to public scrutiny.

Attacking covertly means not pursuing targets that serve the public (or private groups sufficiently large that having everyone remain silent is unlikely). Eligible targets are those that belong to parts of the government or to internal systems of institutions permitted and likely to keep matters private. Two ironies follow. One is that the best targets of sub-rosa cyberattacks are those whose workings are not only hidden but whose existence target states are reluctant to admit in the first place.[39] That noted, many such systems tend to be air-gapped and thus very hard targets. The other is that open societies, such as the United States, do not offer good targets for a sub-rosa attack because of the difficulty of keeping such attacks secret in such societies. Closed societies offer more good targets for sub-rosa attacks. Similarly, because

---

[39] In the wake of the controversy over the Defense Advanced Research Project Agency's Total Information Awareness program, funding was ended. If, as many believe, the program went underground into the intelligence community, those that run such systems may be quite reluctant to admit that they exist.

secrecy is emphasized in war, states at war offer more sub-rosa targets than those at peace.[40]

There is, incidentally, a world of difference between a deterrence strategy that assumes a public response and the option to go public. Threatening to go public with an act of escalation that may affect public opinion (e.g., by its audacity) *after the fact* is like relinquishing the steering wheel to an enraged public.[41] Once the crisis starts, however, the national security elite would be acting against type to relinquish that sort of control.[42]

Managing the Third-Party Problem

Escalation-management strategies also have to contend with the problem of distinguishing attacks by third parties from those of the adversary. One saving grace is that the third-party problem is different in wartime. Against a background of full-bore cyberattacks, third parties have to make a larger splash than they do in peacetime to be considered escalation. In peacetime, a state that has been attacked in cyberspace and does nothing has to explain to its public and foreign observers why. In wartime, it can credibly argue that it is already doing all it can against the adversary and that a failure to escalate is not a display of cowardice. Because each side will naturally assume that its enemy on the battlefield is responsible for the escalatory cyberattack, the third parties do not have to strain to imitate the signature of a particular state. Even if there are doubts, the state that is the target of the third party is more likely to respond as if attacked by its battlefield foe if it reasons that doing so will not create a new enemy. Conversely, the possibility that escalation could have been carried out by third parties cre-

---

[40] There may be other bureaucratic reasons that the sub-rosa character of the operations remains. Inertia is one. The reluctance to declassify what were previously highly classified activities is another.

[41] Schelling, 1960.

[42] Leslie H. Gelb and Richard K. Betts, *The Irony of Vietnam: The System Worked*, Washington, D.C.: Brookings Institution, 1979.

ates an excuse for *not* counterescalating, even for an adversary's attack, until attribution is sorted out.

Third parties can create crises in wartime in ways unavailable in peacetime. A cyberattack on a strategic system (which should be nearly impossible but is conceivable) may be considered inexplicable in peacetime. A similar attack in wartime could be considered a precursor to escalation from conventional to strategic because such escalation is quite plausible. Fortunately, because the easy targets will have already been taken offline or hardened early in a war and the harder targets will require considerable preparation, early participation by third parties may be relatively ineffectual. Over time, however, serious third parties can contribute a larger percentage of the total mischief if they take the time to focus on the target system, deepening their understanding of it, and looking patiently for vulnerabilities.

If escalation management requires controlling third parties, two questions arise: First, how can states determine whether attacks came from third parties rather than adversaries? Second, and far trickier, how can states prevent their adversaries from mistaking third-party attacks for their own attacks, particularly escalatory ones?

Determining who carried out an attack—a third party or the battlefield foe—uses some of the same techniques such a question would require in peacetime. In wartime, an attacker's access is both worse and better: worse because there are fewer day-to-day contacts, and better because some of the entry points may come from proximity to military conflict (e.g., an enemy UAV transmitter/receiver penetrating the battlefield). Furthermore, because the adversary is likely to be carrying out a larger number of attacks in wartime, particularly on military forces, there should be a larger body of evidence from which to distinguish the adversary's modus operandi from those of third parties.[43] Defenders can choose to distinguish attacks by battlefield foes from others by reasoning that their foes have no interest in wasting

---

[43] If the third party is attacking precisely to create further mischief between adversaries, what prevents it from copying one side's modus operandi as part of the ruse? The answer may be stated as a question: Can one copy a well-known modus operandi (which, having been used, has already set defenses against it in motion) and still carry out a successful attack?

their assets, notably their knowledge of the opponents' vulnerabilities, on low-impact attacks; thus, low-impact attacks are likely to have been carried out by others.

It is not easy to keep third-party attacks from inducing an adversary reaction. Warring parties rarely overflow with mutual trust. Having each side monitor the other's cyberwarriors to ensure that their attacks are limited in scope is not possible for an activity that requires deception to work.

If dealing with a foe that is less sophisticated and likely to overreact to cyberattacks against sensitive systems, one could monitor and immunize their systems against the attacks of others—that is, firewall such systems to ensure that no third parties get through. This may sound far-fetched, but some forms of the malware that convert systems into bots make it difficult for third parties to insert their own malware into such systems. If that is unappealing, a state can at least tell adversaries that some of their sensitive systems (that it does not intend to attack) have vulnerabilities so that they attend to such vulnerabilities before third parties exploit them. However, *finding* such vulnerabilities would require spying on such systems, which may itself raise suspicions.

The Need for a Clean Shot

The problems of intrawar deterrence are similar in many respects to those of interwar deterrence, insofar as the *threat* to retaliate will work only if the adversary

- believes that it will be blamed[44]
- believes that the target has the means to carry out the deterrent threat

---

[44] This is a much smaller problem for intrawar deterrence because the usual reason to not respond in peacetime is the fear of starting a war—but, if the war has already started, such a fear is limited to the fear of the other side escalating.

- believes that the target has the will to carry out the deterrent threat even if it threatens to counter the target's reprisals with reprisals of its own
- believes that, if it does *not* cross a red line, it will not face escalation
- feels that its escalation has no compelling rationale that persuades it that it is militarily better off having escalated even after taking the target's potential response into account[45]
- does not fear losing too much face by complying (which argues for making such a threat implicitly or covertly)
- believes that the red lines are well-defined, straightforward to monitor, and considered fair—rather than one-sided, arbitrary, unfounded in customary law, or self-serving.

This is clearly a list of nontrivial length and content. Just as clearly, the success of a tit-for-tat strategy of intrawar deterrence has everything to do with what the other side believes. Thus, those that would adopt such a strategy have to have a fairly good read of the other side.

The problems do not end there if a state declares or strongly implies a tit-for-tat strategy and has defined red lines, and it is attacked anyway. It will have to either respond or give a good show of why it did not. It can claim that what the other side did was not escalatory by, somewhat incredibly, pretending that it did not cross a threshold or that it is unsure who did what and hope that the adversary does not take credit.[46] If that claim is unconvincing, the state may have to either

---

[45] This better-off logic does not apply in peacetime because a stand-alone cyberwar, incapable of destroying very much for very long, ends up becoming a battle of pain-making and pain tolerance and hence tends toward the mutually unsatisfactory when both sides weigh in. Thus, the prospects for peacetime deterrence, as problematic as it is, at least has some of the calculus in its favor compared with intrawar cyberdeterrence, in which mutual escalation can actually leave one side better off on the battlefield.

The target's potential response is particularly important if the worst possible reaction in cyberspace is a tolerable price to pay. This is no guarantee, however, that the target will not respond violently, if it can.

[46] That is, if one side wants to avoid having to respond to escalation by pretending that it was a third party that carried out an attack that crossed a red line (or would have crossed a red

escalate when prudence would dictate otherwise or do nothing and lose credibility.

Inference and Narrative

Escalation, by definition, is doing something different today from what one has done before. It leads to speculation about whether the adversary's intentions have changed or are different from once thought. Similarly, a state's failure to respond to escalation also gives rise to speculation about its attitudes.

Consider how a state's response to its adversary's cyberescalation may be read. What might others infer from a state's responding to cyberescalation with escalation of its own?

- The attack was detected and attributed correctly—a nontrivial achievement. A corruption attack or a destruction attack against a little-used but nevertheless critical function, such as backup, may go undetected.
- The state *can* escalate—also nontrivial. It means that the state has the technical know-how to breach barriers associated with targets that were previously untouched.
- The state *would* escalate. The state is not afraid of escalation; it cannot be cowed. Additionally, whatever inhibitions it had against hitting a class of targets no longer exists.
- The initial attack hurt or embarrassed the target state enough to convince it to carry out cyberattacks of the sort that it previously did not want or need to do. Or the discomfort was so great that the target state would escalate to really painful points in order to create a clear deterrent against carrying out such attacks.

---

line had its adversary carried it out), its strategy would be frustrated if the adversary stood up and claimed, "I did it!" That would put pressure on the target to respond.

- The state does not like risking casualties by responding kinetically, so it responds only in cyberspace.[47]
- The state is cruel and vicious, particularly if the response crosses red lines the adversary had yet to breach. It therefore must be heeded or, alternatively, destroyed.

The first three responses flatter the responding state as, respectively, adept on forensics, capable on offense, and steadfast. The last three point to a state that is, respectively, oversensitive, cowardly, and thuggish.

All this assumes that the retaliating state was, in fact, responding to an attack by the entity against which it retaliated. If no such attack took place, the state may be viewed as twitchy, trigger-happy, and ultimately incompetent. If an attack took place but from another entity, the state's confidence in its own attribution systems would be deemed misplaced. Or the attacker may convince itself that the retaliating state is dishonest about why it escalated and was just looking for an excuse (particularly if no such precipitating and escalatory attack took place).

Correspondingly, a state that failed to respond may allow the reverse implications to be drawn. That is, the state could not detect the attack, could detect the attack but was unsure who did it, or could not respond successfully. The state may have been cowed into not responding. Alternatively, it would not breach its ethical norms to respond, or it could afford to let such an attack pass.

The broad narrative that a state has used to frame its cyberspace policy may color its response options. A narrative that assumes bad things in cyberspace largely because systems are complex and fragile buys a state some time to consider its options after an attack. A corollary narrative that focuses on the faults of the defense rather than the fiendishness of the offense also makes it easier to avoid counterescalation.

The target state could make it appear that it retaliated when it did not. It could announce that its hackers have been unleashed (pre-

---

[47] Suppose that X attacks Y. Y responds but only in cyberspace. X infers that Y is a coward when it comes to violence, but X's inference is unfounded if Y just did not think that the damage from the attack rose to the level of justifying violence.

sumably, hackers had been leashed earlier). Faking a kinetic attack is very difficult, but faking a cyberattack is not because nearly everything about it is hidden. Such a stratagem would be the opposite of a sub-rosa response, and the claimed retaliatory attack would have to have non-obvious effects (e.g., corruption rather than disruption). An opponent that believes this may well divert resources to calculating which of its information stores or algorithms have been tampered with. What it concludes if it finds something suspicious—for any number of other reasons—is another issue.

Should a state, then, escalate based on what its opponents succeed in doing or on what they tried to do? If the purpose of escalation management is to inhibit what foes try to do rather than what they succeed in doing, then attempts alone suffice for a response. Yet, successful attacks illuminate intent much better than failed ones do: An armed man caught entering a building may clearly have been up to no good, but who was his target, and was his intent murder, assault, or intimidation? Furthermore, not only is the public unlikely to know of failed attempts, but, in some circumstances, the foe may be unsure why the attempt failed and thus may not be sure that the attempt registered with the target. So, the target loses less face when not responding to a failed attack.

States inclined toward retaliation may need to explain why particular targets that are out of bounds for kinetic attack are fair game for cyberattack (e.g., when is an attack on a port that supports operations in an offshore theater island *not* prefatory to an invasion of the adversary's homeland?).[48] The next question is obvious: Why would the victim state believe such a state, particularly if the attacking state

---

[48] Although a state could announce that it is eyeing a particular target system in order to elicit from the target any reason that such an attack should not be carried out, will the target use such warning to bulwark or isolate such systems or scream very loudly in the hopes that it can be spared even though nothing particularly critical was at stake? Would the target even find such a request legitimate? See, e.g., Lincoln P. Bloomfield, Jr., "National Security Fundamentals in the Space and Cyber Domains," *High Frontier*, Vol. 7, No. 1, November 2010, pp. 34–38.

There is no assurance that clear messaging at the leadership level between the United States and the adversary would serve as a brake on escalation in such a situation; but the absence of such communication would leave each side with no incentive or excuse for restraint.

suspects that the *only* purpose of any announcement would be to gain some military or strategic advantage? One answer may be that ancillary actions prefatory to a general escalation are absent. But that presupposes that the target of retaliation *can detect* such ancillary actions well enough to know that the cyberattack had a limited purpose, when a key purpose of any cyberattack is to persuade the adversary to doubt its information. So, whereas the problem of explaining escalation is not unique to cyberwar,[49] the use of cyberwar makes all explanations all the more suspect.

Inferences are even harder to draw when states are not unitary actors.[50] One bureaucratic faction in a warring state may carry out cyberattacks to rally the state's population behind its particular bent, say, in favor of greater belligerence, or against its particular *bête noire* (to take on country A when others want to take on country B).[51] Although kinetic attacks, particularly the larger ones, can be traced back, the source of a cyberattack may remain mysterious for a long time. Even leaders who seek calm can be frustrated by the difficulty of enforcing their writ on their minions—and, because a capacity for cyberwar needs only hackers, sufficiently detailed intelligence on the target, and a modicum of hardware, factions may have the requisite power to create considerable mischief. Retaliation by the target may well play

---

[49] As argued in Walter B. Slocombe, "Preplanned Operations," in Ashton B. Carter, John D. Steinbruner, and Charles A. Zraket, eds., *Managing Nuclear Operations*, Washington, D.C.: Brookings Institution, 1987, pp. 121–141, "How do you convince the other side that one's limited attacks are, in fact, limited?"

[50] Is China, for instance, a unified actor?

> [China's President Hu Jintao's] strange encounter with Defense Secretary Robert M. Gates here last week—in which [Hu] was apparently unaware that his own air force had just test-flown China's first stealth fighter—was only the latest case suggesting that he has been boxed in or circumvented by rival power centers. (David E. Sanger and Michael Wines, "China Leader's Limits Come into Focus as U.S. Visit Nears," *New York Times*, January 16, 2011)

[51] Japan's army circa 1941 was more interested in combat with China and perhaps Russia, while Japan's navy had its eye on the West's colonies in South and Southeast Asia and thus was itching to go after the UK and the United States. The United States in the 1790s found itself divided between factions that favored France and those that favored its wartime enemy, Britain.

into the hands of the aggressive rather than the more cautious faction; the former can display it as proof of the target's hostile nature. In such circumstances, the target state must ask, would the positive deterrence effect from counterescalation trump the negative effect from confirming the narrative of the more aggressive faction? If not, the target state may prefer to let the incident pass.

Command and Control

C2 arrangements color escalation management in all forms of combat, but nowhere more so than in cyberspace. The problem arises with both the commanders and those they command.

Commanders

Will commanders act appropriate to the crises, follow standard operating procedures, or enhance institutional interests? As Barry Posen, for instance, observed, "During the Cuban Missile Crisis, the U.S. Navy ran its blockade according to its traditional methods, disregarding President Kennedy's instructions," adding "orders to cease U-2 flights near the Soviet border were either not received, or were ignored; Soviet detection of these flights hindered the negotiations to end this crisis."[52] George Smoke argued that one of the reasons that Britain found itself mired in the Crimean War was that it perceived that Russia's devastating defeat of the Turkish fleet at Sinope was meant as an insult to the British themselves.[53] Britain implied that it would not respond if the Russians fought at sea as long as they did not attack a Turkish port. The czar concluded from this that naval action was acceptable as long as it took place at sea. But Russian admirals interpreted matters consistently with their desires and carried out their actions within the port of Sinope (without actually attacking the port facilities themselves). All that noted, cyberoperations do not have the long history of naval

---

[52] Barry R. Posen, "Inadvertent Nuclear War? Escalation and NATO's Northern Flank," *International Security*, Vol. 7, No. 2, Autumn 1982, pp. 28–54, pp. 32, 34.

[53] Smoke, 1997, p. 182.

operations. Whatever standard operating procedures exist are yet to be validated in a war or crisis against a competent enemy.

The influence of the cyberwarrior community's drive for status and recognition may play a large role. Like the U.S. Army Air Forces in the 1940s, cyberwarriors may wish to be seen as part of a military organization capable of creating strategic effects rather than just supporting other warfighters.[54] In a war, would they see more value in using their limited set of exploits against strategic targets? Would they disdain operations against military targets (that normally present little escalation risk if they can be engaged by kinetic means) in favor of strategic operations that carry a nontrivial risk of escalation?

The role of cyberwarriors within the regional combatant commands (COCOMs) colors the question for the United States. If, for instance, cyberwarriors were organized as teams reporting to a warfighting organization, such as an army division or even a regional combatant commander, then the subordination of community prerogatives to the total fight would more likely follow. In the United States, however, regional commands do not "own" cyberwarriors. All cyberoperations come under the C2 of USCYBERCOM, whose units are *not* chopped to combatant commanders but exercised directly.[55] USCYBERCOM reports to USSTRATCOM, whose other primary mission is nuclear and space forces. As LTG Keith Alexander emphasized,

> The Commander of U.S. Cyber Command will have freedom of action to conduct military operations in cyberspace based upon the authorities provided by the President, the Secretary of Defense, and the Commander, U.S. Strategic Command. Because cyberspace is not generally bounded by geography, the Commander of U.S. Cyber Command will have to *coordinate* with U.S. agencies

---

[54] Cyberwarriors have not pressed to become their own corps, much less their own service. Although we put forth the case for a separate information corps nearly 20 years ago, the purpose of such a corps was to generate a joint picture of the battlefield based on the coordinated operation and analysis of sensors, not to carry out information warfare (as it was then called). See Martin C. Libicki and James A. Hazlett, "Do We Need an Information Corps?" *Joint Forces Quarterly*, Vol. 2, Autumn 1993, pp. 88–97.

[55] *Chopping* a unit means to allow a unit under one's command to work for another commander for the time being.

and Combatant Commanders that would be affected by actions taken in cyberspace.[56]

Hence the question, current authorities notwithstanding, who ought to determine what cyberoperations are carried out during a military crisis or war? Institutional factors cannot be ignored.[57] In a war or military crisis, only USCYBERCOM will really know whether worthwhile strategic targets have vulnerabilities that can be exploited and to what effect, whereas the existence of kinetic targets is easier to demonstrate (e.g., by imagery). Insider knowledge may influence the options that the U.S. cyber commander presents to the regional COCOMs, if the latter get to select at all. Otherwise, a U.S. cyber commander may well select targets and take risks (or avoid taking them) that are inconsistent with how regional commanders would fight, if indeed the latter understand the risks and rewards of operations in cyberspace with sufficient detail at all. Yet it is the regional commanders who are the more knowledgeable about the most important factor in escalation management, the other side: what it thinks, what it infers about the U.S. posture, and where its red lines are drawn.[58] If USSTRATCOM backs up the cyber commander's subordinate commander (even that is unnecessary if the U.S. cyber commander becomes a combatant commander in his or her own right) when there are disagreements over targeting and operational procedures, the Secretary of Defense (SecDef) would have to arbitrate. Under such circumstances, regional commanders may not wish cyber to be the issue that gets raised to that level, particularly because the U.S. cyber commander will be the sole source of the details required to resolve the balance of risk and reward. Furthermore, requiring SecDef intervention will almost certainly slow the pace of battle.

---

[56] Alexander, 2010, p. 14. Emphasis added.

[57] See also U.S. Government Accountability Office, *Defense Department Cyber Efforts: More Detailed Guidance Needed to Ensure Military Services Develop Appropriate Cyberspace Capabilities*, Washington, D.C., GAO-11-421, May 2011.

[58] By contrast, the close relationship between USCYBERCOM and the National Security Agency (NSA) reduces the odds that intelligence gain/loss considerations will be ignored when attacks on targets threaten to reveal penetrations to the target, the fixing of which jeopardizes taps into systems that produce intelligence.

Escalation management also has to account for the power of the cyberwarrior community to force action when inaction may be called for. Consider that holes, once they are revealed to the defender, tend to be closed quickly. A cyberwarrior, on a limited mission, could exploit a vulnerability, discover that its exploitation can have vast if not necessarily precisely scoped effects, and beg for the authority to pursue action lest the vulnerability close forever. Active defense—in the sense of prompt action against machines on the attack—also presents opportunities for light-speed reaction that could lead to escalation that a little contemplation can foresee and forestall. The problem, of course, is worse, if the cyberwarriors are deliberately heedless of bounds on their actions, an issue covered next.

All this argues for two propositions. First, combatant commanders should have full control over cyberoperations whether or not they are deemed operational or strategic, if for no other reason so that their escalatory effects can be factored into the overall campaign plan.[59] Second, it may be useful for the United States to keep its cyberwar community under commands whose primary mission is the application of kinetic force, the better to remind everyone that cyberoperations exist to further the political ends—which, as Carl von Clausewitz observed, are the justifications for kinetic operations as well.[60]

Those They Command

States that would manage escalation in cyberspace must have appropriate C2 of their cyberwarriors. Instructions on what to avoid must be clear, and the controls must be in place to ensure that such instructions are followed.

In the physical world, both command and control are getting better thanks to ever-more-ubiquitous surveillance and the proliferation of communication networks. The effects of war can be meticu-

---

[59] This does not imply that the regional commander would have access to all the tools possessed by USCYBERCOM because it may be advantageous to hold some tricks in reserve so they can be available for their greatest need, which may not necessarily be in the theater of operations at the time.

[60] Carl von Clausewitz, *On War*, Princeton, N.J.: Princeton University Press, 1989.

lously documented and attributed.[61] As more military equipment becomes digitized and thus capable of hosting copious log files, the prospect of knowing exactly who did what and when draws closer.

Not so in the cyberworld, in which keystrokes can come from anywhere. Standard operating procedures are a poor guide when one cannot say a priori exactly what the means of attack are, much less what the likely effects of attacks are. Any policy designed to attack up to some boundary but no further is subject to the two aforementioned differences: between intent and effect and between effect and perception. If one would act, clear and *thick* (to account for misunderstandings) margins of some sort have to be established.

The burden of margin-setting will differ depending on whether one is worried about careful, careless, or rogue cyberwarriors.

Careful cyberwarriors are those that pay as much attention to constraints as they do to results. For them, clarity is the goal. The constraints on their behavior could include how to attack and what results are wanted and unwanted under which circumstances. The bounds should be explicit, advertised, and stable against arbitrary change. The rules that say what actions are permissible in what situations should be codified in advance of crisis because, when the fighting starts, purposes are more fluid and not necessarily obvious to all. To make constraints work, it may be necessary to teach the basic principles of cyberwar as they apply to national security. Beyond such guidelines, however, the rules on how to attack or what constitutes nonexcessive damage may be too context-specific to be specific in advance.

Careless cyberwarriors mean to follow the rules but, in the heat of combat, may convince themselves that carrying out a clear operational mission trumps conformance with inevitably ambiguous guidelines. All the rules for careful cyberwarriors apply to careless ones, and the two may be indistinguishable. The application may vary: The actions of careless warriors are likely to drift over the borders, and, being human,

---

[61] Martin C. Libicki, David C. Gompert, David R. Frelinger, and Raymond Smith, *Byting Back—Regaining Information Superiority Against 21st-Century Insurgents: RAND Counterinsurgency Study—Volume 1*, Santa Monica, Calif.: RAND Corporation, MG-595/1-OSD, 2007, Chapter Four.

such warriors are likely to blame their trespasses on unclear guidance, the ambiguities of cyberspace, and even the target's behavior (e.g., turning off the electric power substation to disable government bureaus was not supposed to put hospital patients at risk; where were the latter's backup generators?). If careless cyberwarriors are a problem, one approach would be to limit the amount of intelligence with which *all* cyberwarriors are provided (e.g., avoid probing systems that will never be targets). But, given a wide enough range of contexts, what systems can one aver will *never* be targets?

Rogue warriors are those so eager to strike the target that they take their work home with them, sometimes literally. Trained and filled with intelligence at work, they carry out attacks from platforms or intermediate conduits that are very difficult to trace and out of sight of their supervisors. Rogue warriors will not respond to constraints when freelancing except as warnings about what to avoid appearing to do. Because they do not have to work in military formations or with unique military hardware, their operations are harder to detect and hence control than their equivalents in physical combat (e.g., the militias of developing nations). Not even keeping them chained to their desks in a military crisis will eliminate mischief if they have found how to contact their own bots from their desktop—although such behavior may be suppressed if they have to account for every keystroke. Effective militaries have ways of filtering out most such rogue warriors and engineering social controls that keep potential rogue warriors in the force from straying. Having done what they can, states then have to determine whether the risks of violating self-imposed constraints merit reducing every cyberwarrior's access to the intelligence and tools necessary to mount the more-sophisticated attacks.

Conclusions

A state that would limit wartime cyberattacks against its society and out-of-theater military must pay attention to cyberescalation.[62] Avoiding escalation may be simpler if a war's goals are limited and actions follow accordingly. But fine-grained escalation management in cyberspace will remain tricky because of the difficult coupling between intentions, effects, and perceptions.

Escalation in cyberwar—particularly if cyber against cyber—is likely to be jerky rather than smooth. The kind of escalation presented by Herman Kahn, in which both sides feel their way up the proverbial escalation ladder to see who breaks first, is unlikely to characterize cyberwar (whether it characterizes any war is a separate question). What looks like a carefully calibrated ladder may, in practice, end up as a hodgepodge of sticky and bouncy rungs.[63] Thus, although Figure 4.2 shows a multistep ladder in the absence of well-defined and agreed-upon thresholds, a few large moves are more likely. Perhaps there will be only one escalation phase—from the unproblematic use of cyberattacks in an operational context against military targets, to an entirely problematic set of attacks that have or appear to have a strategic and coercive rationale against civilian targets.[64] Alternatively, the only attacks that may be deemed seriously escalatory are those that cross the border between instrumental (tactical) and general (strategic) or from legitimate to illegitimate. That, in turn, presupposes norms of what is one and what is the other, and such norms do not exist now and may not exist anytime soon.

Unlike other forms of warfare, the first use of a serious cyberattack could easily make states realize that the security-versus-convenience

---

[62] Because cyberattacks may lead to kinetic escalation, the importance of escalation management is not limited to the virtual realm.

[63] Sticky rungs are those from which one cannot rise; bouncy rungs are those from which one rises much farther than anticipated.

[64] Imagine a scenario in which the regional combatant commander makes an urgent request that a SAM site be knocked out. The cyber commander sees no way to get into the SAM site but knows that a "small" attack on the local power supply may have the same effect. The other side finds this "small" attack escalatory. And so on.

trade-off had tilted too far to convenience;[65] they will thus harden themselves quickly, making future cyberattacks more difficult. A cyberattacker that understands as much will necessarily want to front-load attacks knowing that attacks postponed are attacks denied. Furthermore, the *perceived* effects of cyberattacks tend to be more unpredictable than the effects of kinetic attacks.[66]

Proxy conflicts are particularly hazardous from the perspective of controlling crises by keeping matters in theater. The many potential third parties each have their own agendas, and physical boundaries are a relatively poor delineation of what is or is not a legitimate target. Nevertheless, both sides could take caution to isolate systems they put into theater from home systems, and each should remember that accidents happen. Wisdom also suggests postponing action against third parties, however annoying they may be.

States should also take the time to consider escalation carefully. There is little to be gained from an instant response. Cyberattacks cannot disarm another side's ability to respond in kind. True, cyberattacks cannot be frozen to be thawed out when needed; maintenance requires recurrent surveillance. But the timing of a response ought to be predicated on one's warfighting strategy, not a desire for speed-of-light responses.

Each state should also understand the other side's reaction to cyberescalation, notably what ethical norms it associates with cyberattacks vis-à-vis kinetic attacks and what others may infer about the attacker's intentions from such attacks. In cyberspace, as in other realms of warfare, "the defender frequently does not understand how threatening his behavior, though defensively motivated, may seem to the other side."[67]

---

[65] So, is the security-versus-convenience trade-off ipso facto tilted away from security? Perhaps necessarily; perhaps everyone has it right and no devastating cyberattacks are in the offing. More likely, some have tilted one way and some the other, and a major incident will excite the security laggards disproportionately.

[66] That noted, the psychological impact of the perceived effect has large random error terms for both kinetic and cyberwarfare.

[67] Posen, 1982, p. 33.

CHAPTER FIVE

Implications for Strategic Stability

Cyberwar is said to present stability problems similar to those associated with nuclear weapons. Not for nothing did a summer 2010 cover story in the *Economist* picture cyberwar as the digital equivalent of the nuclear bomb, a threat to civilization that necessitated international negotiations and arms control. But does cyberwar threaten strategic stability? Although the matter is still not settled,[1] this chapter argues that the factors that make nuclear instability an issue do not apply in cyberspace, or at least not in the same way.

If the definition of *strategic stability* is widened to include all possible sources of inadvertent war, we argue, cyberwar has created new ways to stumble into war that largely arise from error and misperception on one side exacerbated by hypervigilance on the other.

Finally, we discuss the advantages to strategic stability and risks of managing cybercrises by operating entirely sub rosa—where the effects of attacks and hence their existence are known only by the attackers and the defenders, not by third parties or publics at large.

Translating Sources of Cold War Instability to Cyberspace

The quest for strategic stability was a leitmotiv of the Cold War thinking. Worry about whether the Soviet Union could disable U.S. nuclear deterrence with a first strike shaped the U.S. nuclear posture in the late

---

[1] As General Alexander testified (Alexander, 2010, p. 17), "A consensus has yet to emerge, either on how to characterize the strategic 'instability' or what to do about it."

1950s and gave impetus to concerns about a "window of vulnerability" in the late 1970s. Arguments for and against the antiballistic missile or strategic arms limitations often cited their putative effects on strategic stability in the early 1970s and throughout the 1980s. Fears of unstable reactions pervaded planning for nuclear C2, as well as indication and warning systems.

Although nuclear arms are still with us, issues associated with strategic stability have migrated from the nuclear arena to the new arena of cyberspace. The fear is that systemic factors in the environment tend to drive states toward rather than away from conflict—notably, but not exclusively, conflict that neither state intended. In an unstable environment, chance factors may cause some states to react in ways that bring out reactions from other states that reinforce mutual fear. The prisoner's dilemma is the unstable situation created when states in crises must each decide whether to strike first or hold off. In World War I, the inflexibility of railroad schedules supposedly played a role in the alacrity with which both sides mobilized lest they found themselves outgunned on the front at the outset.

To gauge the instabilities induced by the possibility of cyberwar, we pose several questions by way of comparison.

What Influence Can Cyberwar Have If Nuclear Weapons Exist?

Although the Cold War is over, nuclear weapons are still with us, and that fact limits the amount of strategic instability arising from cyberspace. Nuclear-armed countries may choose to yield to the will of another state, but they cannot be annihilated or taken over except at a cost that would exceed anything that cyberwar can promise. Even forced regime change may be off the table. To date, cyberwar has yet to claim its first life. In other words, a state with nuclear weapons that is worried largely about the survival of the nation and its citizens can afford to ignore whatever relative superiority its rivals enjoy in cyberspace alone. Of greater import is the extent to which cyberwar skills can establish or exacerbate a state's superiority in the application of kinetic force. Even if a state still has to worry about the damage such attacks can cause, the stakes, although potentially large, are less than existential.

Can a Cyberattack Disarm a Target State's Nuclear Capabilities?

Although cyberattacks could, in theory, create serious instability by altering the terms of a nuclear standoff, it is hard to believe that protecting networks against vulnerabilities could rise beyond the level of yet another thing to keep in mind when designing a nuclear establishment. Operations in cyberspace are rarely capable of breaking things. True, whoever created the Stuxnet worm apparently shortened the lifespan of Iran's nuclear centrifuges, but this was active machinery already subject to computer commands, which were then interfered with.[2] Nuclear weapons, by contrast, spend most of their time doing nothing while waiting for a go signal. Conceivably, one state could hack into the nuclear command system of another state, render its weapons unusable, and use the temporary monopoly of power to coerce its target. But states are extraordinarily cautious in the construction of their nuclear establishments and give primary C2 and its various secondary backups a great deal of thought.[3] Even technologically unsophisticated states retain very simple but robust ways of wielding their nuclear weapons if everything else fails; indeed, their lack of sophistication suggests they use such a strategy. Furthermore, it is unclear how the aggressor state would *know* that its cyberoperations had, in fact, disabled the target state's ability to fire its nuclear weapons. Its hackers may have disconnected everything they saw, but how confident would they be that they saw everything? There could be several duplicated paths, each separate

---

[2] The fact that so many centrifuges were destroyed but that the production of enriched uranium did not decline has suggested to some that the affected units were in their early stages of being installed into the centrifuge cascades—that is, the point at which their parameters are being adjusted by the infected computer controllers. Conversely, by this argument, centrifuges whose parameters were already established appear to have been less affected by Stuxnet if at all. A corresponding analogy may be that installed nuclear weapons are much less vulnerable to the type of cyberattack that plagued Natanz; only those whose parameters are being adjusted are that vulnerable.

[3] Even criticisms of nuclear C2 arrangements cite the complexity of efforts the United States uses to ensure that they always are available. On a somewhat different note, the 1983 movie *War Games*, besides offering a cautionary tale against nuclear war in general and automation of military functions in particular, also suggested that connecting nuclear command systems to modem banks is inadvisable.

from the other. C2 software, unlike missile silos or submarine pens, is invisible from space.

Now consider the possibility that the target state's nuclear weapons are not destroyed but only disconnected for a while. Unless the aggressor can quickly follow up and permanently disarm the target state's nuclear capacity kinetically (in which case, the nuclear standoff alone could be unstable, with or without cyberwar), the target state need only stall for enough time to reconnect its weapons in order to reestablish its deterrence. If the aggressor tries to carry out operations of the sort that might meet nuclear retaliation were such capabilities intact, the target state might credibly retort that retaliation, if delayed, is nevertheless coming. The aggressor might then reason that, when the time comes, retaliation will be less likely by virtue of its having been thought out. After all, by then, the prospect of unthinking retaliation that may arise by chance à la Schelling is greatly reduced, and, at that point, the purpose of retaliation will be compellence and hence more likely to be resisted, leading to a possible counterstrike from the aggressor, if necessary, to back up the threat. But the aggressor would be taking a big chance by acting on that logic.

What may be more unstable is not the results of the attack but the revealed intention of one state to disarm another state's ultimate weapon, even if only temporarily. This could alter the target state's view of the attacker's intentions—and that *might* lead to a crisis.

Can a Cyberattack Disarm a Target State's Cyberwarriors?

The prospect that a state that strikes first can, by so doing, create an overwhelming presumption in favor of ultimate victory is highly unstable. The nuclear era was pervaded by the fear that one side would find that it could substantially degrade the other side's retaliatory capability through a first strike. The victimized state would be either completely disarmed or so denuded of strike power that it would not credibly strike back without risking the destruction of its cities to no useful strategic end. The discovery, in the mid-1950s, that the strategic posture of the

United States might one day lend itself to being disarmed by a first strike had a profound effect on nuclear planning.[4]

By contrast, cyberwar cannot disarm cyberwarriors. The reason is simple. The ability to carry out cyberwar requires no more than four inputs: clever hackers, intelligence on the target's operations and vulnerabilities, a computing device, and network connections.[5] Cyberwar, clearly, cannot destroy the first two. Cyberattacks against an unprepared computer sitting on the network at the time—two less-than-universal conditions—may disable it temporarily but rarely destroy it.[6] Such computers can be rebooted, or, at worst, returned to factory conditions within hours; new ones cost no more than a few hundred dollars these days. The threat to end network connections to the target country, although very difficult to carry out in practice, is at least a theoretical possibility. However, any serious cyberwar-capable state has probably figured out how to carry out cyberattacks starting from someone else's territory or, better yet, from within the territory of the country it is targeting.[7] It would not be unreasonable to assume that many cyberwar-capable states have placed hackers overseas or at least

---

[4] The touchstone public article is Albert Wohlstetter, "The Delicate Balance of Terror," *Foreign Affairs*, Vol. 37, No. 2, January 1959, pp. 211–223; this article was, in part, based on an analysis of U.S. bomber basing in the mid-1950s.

[5] In such cases as Flame, in which cryptography is involved, it helps to have available sufficient computing resources; see Dan Goodin, "Crypto Breakthrough Shows Flame Was Designed by World-Class Scientists," *Ars Technica*, June 7, 2012. However, if the work of these computer resources precedes the deployment of the malware, then destroying them afterward makes little difference to the course of that particular malware attack or of future attacks for which the cryptography has already been worked out.

[6] Apparently, there was a vulnerability in Hewlett-Packard printer software that permitted hackers to raise the fuser temperature high enough to burn paper (Sebastian Anthony, "Tens of Millions of HP LaserJet Printers Vulnerable to Remote Hacking," *ExtremeTech*, November 29, 2011).

[7] Chinese military writings call for cyberattacks against the United States to be launched from within the United States (James Mulvenon, "Information Warfare and China's Cyber-Warfare Capabilities," speech at Carnegie Endowment for International Peace, Washington, D.C., February 10, 2011). More importantly, Chinese authorities believe that the U.S. response would be delayed by bureaucratic squabbling over Titles 18 and 50 of the U.S. Code (law enforcement and intelligence, respectively), not to mention Title 10 (military) authorities.

implanted malware in computers outside them for the sake of convenience, not to mention survivability.

Therefore, if a first strike cannot disarm its intended target, there is no inherent reason to go after the adversary's cyberwar apparatus first because, when the cyberdust clears, the attacker, having destroyed little that cannot be quickly reconstituted, is no better off than before, even relative to its foe. Indeed, it may be worse off a week later. The best cyberattackers come equipped with knowledge of vulnerabilities in their target computers. Many such vulnerabilities are generic (e.g., they affect all computers running a particular class of software). Attackers tend to create enough evidence in the target computer to allow the latter to figure out what kind of vulnerabilities were exploited. Such vulnerabilities then get patched,[8] leaving the attacker with one fewer trick in its arsenal.

A variant on the disarming first strike that may create instability is to carry out a first strike and then render oneself invulnerable to counterattack by quickly cutting off all of one's own connections to the rest of the world. Such a scenario was posited by Richard Clarke and Robert Knake.[9] This seems akin to taking a quick punch at someone and then jumping behind a wall to avoid a counterpunch: Not only has the aggressor isolated itself more than any cyberattack could do, but it has to emerge eventually, at which point it is no less vulnerable. When due account is taken of the likelihood that the effects of most cyberattacks are temporary, the attractiveness of this strategy dwindles further. There is little in this ploy that would convince potential adversaries to preempt such a maneuver by going first. Furthermore, if potential target states anticipate as much, they could engineer a potential response that works within the other side's network even when the drawbridge is raised.

---

[8] The Stuxnet worm used an unprecedented four zero-day vulnerabilities. All have since been patched, two almost instantly.

[9] Clarke and Knake, 2010, pp. 179–218.

Does Cyberwar Lend Itself to Alert-Reaction Cycles?

In analyzing a U.S.-Soviet confrontation (circa 1984), Paul Bracken described how warnings from one side that nuclear activities were possible would make the other side raise its alert level.[10] Raising the alert level led to procedures that would make nuclear weapons more readily usable (e.g., aircrews would be recalled to base, submarines would launch out to sea). The other side would perceive that its rival was moving closer to striking first and would raise *its* alert level, prompting the first side to move even closer to striking. Such a dynamic reflects the world of nuclear warfare, in which (1) the only response to a growing threat is to raise the readiness of one's offense, (2) there is a decided first-strike advantage and (3) many reactions are visible. Yet, as noted, the first-strike advantage in cyberspace is minimal. Furthermore, a great deal of what goes on in cyberspace is not readily visible (and, being invisible, such operations are less likely to engender rapid reactions). Of greatest importance is that, in contrast to nuclear war, raising cyber*defenses* rather than offenses is quite a viable reaction to the heightened threat of cyberwar. Such defenses may include selectively disconnecting systems, disallowing certain services, tightening access controls, or heavily filtering what enters and leaves networks. Although greater defenses might presage a turn to hostilities, the linkage is relatively weak and could be explained away by a third-party cyberthreat,[11] the discovery of a novel threat vector, or simply the belated realization that cyberdefenses need to receive proper attention.

Are Cyberdefenses Inherently Destabilizing?

The relative independence of defense and offense also casts doubt on the destabilization effects of raising defenses in general. A large class of objections over the ballistic-missile defenses hinged on the proposi-

---

[10] Paul Bracken, "Strategic War Termination," in Ashton B. Carter, John D. Steinbruner, and Charles A. Zraket, eds., *Managing Nuclear Operations*, Washington, D.C.: The Brookings Institution, 1987, pp. 197–214.

[11] In the Cold War, the third-party nuclear threat to the United States was far less consequential than the Soviet nuclear threat. Today's cyberwar environment features three comparably competent states, more strong second-tier states, and a serious transnational criminal capability.

tion that a country that had rendered *other countries'* missiles "impotent and obsolete"[12] would be able to attack other nations with impunity and, having achieved that position, would be able to lash out whenever it wished. Analogously, a nation that had perfected the art of cyber-defenses could hold other countries hostage to its offensive cyberwar capability. This proposition also holds little water (even if one ignores the ability of nuclear weapons and even advanced conventional weapons to trump cyberweapons alone). First, good defenses are unlikely to be exclusive to one country. A large part of defense is proper computer hygiene, elements of which are publicly available. Many of the institutions whose systems have to be protected for such a strategy to work are multinationals, and so are the firms with which they contract for security—this is also how security practices proliferate. Finally, hackers that chance on the defenses of others can learn something about what is newly possible (if not necessarily how it became possible). Second, confidence in such defenses may be hard to come by. Cyberwar is one surprise after another—inevitably so, because it depends on the exploitation of vulnerabilities that the hacker has found and that the defender has not (because, if it knew about its own vulnerabilities, it would undoubtedly fix them). What would it take to rest assured that one will not be surprised anymore? Because a state cannot wield such power over other states until it can convince them that its own confidence is merited, rivals could easily conclude that no such confidence is possible in cyberspace. Third, even if the foe is sufficiently fearful to yield to coercion, it may also be sufficiently fearful to make many trade-offs to bolster its own defenses (e.g., by spending money and creating inconvenience to users). It can hope to reach the point at which the worst possible damage it can bear from a cyberattack is below the threshold at which it feels that it must yield to the aggressor state.

Would a Cyberspace Arms Race Be Destabilizing?

Instability may also, in theory, arise from arms races, particularly if they are large enough to bankrupt the participants and start to per-

---

[12] Ronald Reagan, "Address to the Nation on Defense and National Security," Washington, D.C., March 23, 1983.

suade at least one that a confrontation may be worthwhile if the outcome can end the drain on its treasury. In a sense, such a race already exists—not between states but between defense and offense. Even as old vulnerabilities are fixed, new ones keep getting discovered either in old software or in new software (or in new uses for software that violates implicit assumptions about security, e.g., that opening up an email could not introduce malware into one's computer). As antivirus firms scour the web to identify more malware signatures, malware producers have developed morphing technologies that constantly create hitherto-unseen signatures. Such contests would continue even if states had no interest in cyberwar, although the fact that states *are* interested means that additional resources are being poured into both sides of that contest.

Nevertheless, the logic that states have to develop *offensive* cyberweapons because their rivals do has little basis in theory or fact. First, states have little knowledge of exactly what weapons, as such, are in the arsenal of their rivals.[13] Indeed, if they actually knew precisely what weapons their foes had, they might well know what vulnerabilities such weapons targeted and would fix such vulnerabilities, thereby nullifying these weapons. Second, as noted, the best response to an offensive weapon is a defensive weapon, not another offensive weapon. Third, the whole notion of offense-versus-offense requires that the underlying dynamic of attack and retaliation actually makes sense as a warfighting and war-termination strategy. Were that so, deterrence would be primary. But deterrence is a very difficult notion in cyberspace.[14] States wanting to hide their own tracks in a cyberattack have a wealth of ways to do so and, often, more than enough motive.

Incidentally, it is hard to imagine how an arms race in cyberspace could come close to having a major economic impact. The intellectual skills required to compete in this contest are so specialized that states

---

[13] It takes knowledge of the other side's capabilities to make it a race as such ("they did this, so we must do that"). Yet, the question of whether one side's actually getting such knowledge would cause it to accelerate efforts or relax is an empirical question.

[14] As argued in Libicki, 2009, Chapter Three.

will run out of such people well before they run out of money paying them.

Conversely, would arms control contribute very much to strategic stability? Banning cyberweapons requires stretching the concept of *weapon* beyond its bursting point. A cyberattack requires two components: knowledge of the target and its vulnerabilities, and a capability to translate such knowledge into attack methods that succeed while evading detection and deletion. Generally, the first is harder, but knowledge is not per se a weapon in the sense that we think of weapons. Weaponization is the simpler half,[15] and there is a great deal of material in existence that can be used to develop exploitation and weaponization capabilities once vulnerabilities are found. In other words, not only is verification difficult but also the rationale for weapon control is weak.

Cyber arms control may also not provide the crisis stability that nuclear arms control did.[16] If a state is known to lack nuclear weapons or a nuclear weapon program, others can rest assured that it would take years before having to worry about facing such weapons in a crisis. The same cannot be said of cyberweapons because nearly everything about specific offensive cyberwar capabilities is hidden lest knowledge of techniques lead to their neutralization. The knowledge to go from where nothing is visible to where a serious capability exists can be learned or purchased.

---

[15] Analogy may be drawn to nuclear weapon programs. No state that has amassed the requisite fissile material has failed to complete all the other weaponization steps on the way to building a bomb. See Peter D. Zimmerman, "Proliferation: Bronze Medal Technology Is Enough," *Orbis*, Vol. 38, No. 1, Winter 1994, p. 67.

[16] If there were recognized norms that assured each state that its own infrastructure, for instance, would be safe, each might be more relaxed about investing in offensive and defensive cyberwar capabilities because the consequences of failing to keep up would be correspondingly reduced (e.g., neither side would worry about losing power). That noted, would such norms really be reassuring given difficulties in verification coupled with cyberwar's normal secrecy and ambiguity?

Surprise Attack as a Source of Instability

Cyberwar ceases to be a purely cyberspace problem once an attacking state begins to view a successful cyberattack as an opportunity to carry out a successful military operation or even start a war. Indeed, the perception that fighting will yield useful results may be based on the assumption that the preceding cyberattack will tilt the scales in the attacker's favor. This perception is something that the target state needs to discourage. Therein lies a critical distinction. On the one hand, a cyberdefense good enough to discourage all cyberattacks may be impossible and even unnecessary if the damage from such attacks can be contained. Appendix C explains the relationship between cyberdefense and the discouragement of cyberattacks. *However, a cyberdefense good enough to discourage the enemy from planning kinetic attacks on the basis of a successful cyberattack is far more possible and much more necessary.* In a sense, defense plays two roles. It reduces the pressure on the target to respond hastily to a cyberattack because cyberattacks have less impact than kinetic attacks on the ability to carry out operations.[17] Consequently, the demonstration of confidence may reduce the incentive for the aggressor by raising doubts about whether a cyberattack will be militarily productive.

If attackers convince themselves that their *unsuccessful* efforts in cyberspace cannot be traced back to them, they may view an opening cyberattack as a low-risk proposition: If it works well enough, they can follow up with kinetic attacks, and, if it fails to shift the balance of forces sufficiently, no one is the wiser. If the attackers are wrong about their invisibility, however, war or at least crisis may commence.

Because an imbalance created by a cyberattack would likely be temporary, the attacking state would have a limited window of time to take advantage of the imbalance. This fact limits the usefulness of this tactic to operations that can be carried out and completed in a short time window (e.g., Israel's 2007 attack on alleged nuclear facilities in Syria) or at least situations in which the initial exchanges predispose

---

[17] For instance, if an implant were found, it would be easier for the target to take the position that it may have been espionage and was, anyway, no big deal because its detonation would not have caused serious harm.

the course of the conflict (e.g., Israel's vanquishing of Egypt's air force at the outset of the 1967 war).

Alternatively, and dangerously for stability, a state that uses a no-warning attack to gain an advantage in circumstances that do not necessarily promise a quick conclusion may be tempted to force a quick conclusion through the more intensive application of force. Decisions on whether or not to commit force early in a crisis would then tilt toward commitment. Thus, the attacker escalates sooner on the presumption that it has a limited window of opportunity to take advantage of its opponent's confusion. In other words, the use of a tactic or technique (i.e., offensive cyberwar operations) whose success is synergistic with heavy force commitment promotes escalation at the expense of hedging, therefore complicating crisis control.

A vitiating circumstance is that, if the cyberattack does not achieve its objectives, the attacker, if it tried to not reveal itself, is not necessarily committed to following the cyberattack up with a kinetic attack; the defender is, similarly, not obliged to retaliate. This is a luxury not permitted for attack modes whose authorship is obvious. Furthermore, if the purpose of the attack was to thwart the target state's ability to intervene in a crisis involving a third party *and* the defender is sufficiently paralyzed, the target state can pretend that it had no intention of intervening and do so without losing face—again, a luxury not so easily available if the fact and source of the target's paralysis are known.

Unfortunately for stability, the prospect that such a sneak attack cannot shift the balance of kinetic forces very much is no proof that it will not be attempted *and then followed up* irrespective of results. Here are some reasons:

- The leadership of the attacking state does not know the effectiveness of its attacks and commits to war on the presumption that it will succeed.
- Militaries cannot be turned on and off on a dime. If the window of opportunity to take advantage of a successful cyberattack is measured in days, the military must be mobilized before the cyberattack begins. Even if it does not act, its preparations for kinetic war may have to be so obvious by the time the cyberat-

tack starts that it must fight or face fighting. Thus, the decision to carry out a cyberattack presupposes success and a follow-up by a physical attack whether or not the cyberattack succeeded.

- The attacking state may figure that, if it starts with a major cyber-attack, the target state will respond militarily whether or not the cyberattack was damaging. The attacking state concludes that, if any cyberattack leads to kinetic war, outcomes would be more favorable if it started on the offensive rather than the defensive.

- The attacking country's leadership convinces itself that the cyber-attack did succeed irrespective of actual results. Battle damage assessment, especially in cyberspace, is fuzzy under the best of circumstances. Proponents of war may want others to believe that their efforts worked and thus may proclaim success without fear of contradiction.

Hence the dilemma for countries seeking to avoid crises: The perception of vulnerability, even if misplaced, may create a problem.[18]

Misperception as a Source of Crisis

Although the objective factors of cyberwar suggest that strategic instability is not a problem in cyberspace, the subjective factors of cyberwar create paths to inadvertent conflict without comparable counterpart in the physical world. Uncertainties about allowable behavior, misunderstanding defensive preparations, errors in attribution, unwarranted confidence in the other side's inability to attribute, and misunderstanding the norms of neutrality are all potentially sources of instability leading to crisis.

---

[18] Similar problems may arise if the systems of friends are perceived to be vulnerable. How great a problem this is for the United States depends on the likelihood that a kinetic attack on a friend pulls the United States into war. Ironically, the danger is greatest if intervention by the United States is uncertain. If intervention is certain, then the loss in effectiveness in harming the friend's system matters less if U.S. systems survive because most of the punch will come from the United States. If staying out is certain, there is no crisis. What tempts a crisis is a combination of the friend's weakness and the attacker's false confidence that the matter will not concern the United States.

One Side Takes Great Exception to Cyberespionage
Cyberespionage, which, as espionage, is generally not considered a casus belli, can engender crises in several ways. The most direct method is simply that a state gets tired of its systems becoming the playground of another state. It may have communicated its displeasure, but perhaps too discreetly or subtly to be correctly understood. Alternatively, the attacker—more accurately, the state sponsoring the espionage—may not believe that such displeasure is credible. It would be viewed as a departure from norms. It could be viewed as a sop to domestic audiences. So systems are penetrated, the target gets really upset, retaliates, and a crisis is on.

A crisis could arise if cyberspies err. In the attempt, for instance, to insert a back door to facilitate later entry, the hackers change system parameters that, unbeknownst to them, causes a system failure, perhaps with widespread consequences. Or the hackers reset one system parameter after another to investigate how a system works without realizing how sensitive the system is. By way of illustration (but not example because this account is almost certainly false), a recent journal article quoted unnamed intelligence sources as positing that a power outage in Florida in early 2008 was caused by Chinese hackers who were investigating associated networks when they made a mistake.[19] Finally, spies could leave an implant in a system associated with some critical infrastructure. The target state convinces itself that, because the system targeted by the implant contains no information worth stealing, such an implant can only be considered prefatory to a cyberattack, interpreted as an act of war.

Defenses Are Misinterpreted as Preparations for War
One state's defensive preparations may look like offensive preparations, and other states may panic when objective circumstances suggest they take a deep breath instead. Such overreaction is more likely among

---

[19] A field engineer was diagnosing a switch that had malfunctioned at Florida Power and Light's Flagami substation in west Miami. Without authorization, the engineer disabled two levels of relay protection (Florida Power and Light, "FPL Announces Preliminary Findings of Outage Investigation," press release, Juno Beach, Fla., February 29, 2008). See also Shane Harris, "China's Cyber Militia," *National Journal Magazine*, May 31, 2008.

states that do not trust one another, particularly if one or both sides are primed by events outside in the physical world (e.g., terrorist events, disputed elections, border spats, military movements). To wit: In a crisis, people tend to put a darker face on events than they otherwise would.

Indication and warning work differently in cyberspace. A major kinetic attack, for instance, requires a concert of movements (e.g., tanks moving from garrison, leaves canceled, civilians mobilized, supplies surging to the front). Such events must take place many hours and days before conflict if forces are to be ready when war starts. They can be monitored as indicators and warning. By contrast, every state has to develop a set of nonobvious indicators that suggest that someone is going to attack in cyberspace. If such states thought things through, they might realize that they need not be so eager to respond; everyone with a first-strike potential also has a second-strike potential. But states are not always wise about such matters and may start a crisis or even attempt preemption needlessly.

In practice, preparations for *eventual* cyberattack are almost indistinguishable from preparations for *imminent* cyberattack. Attacks have to be prepared, perhaps years in advance, and cost only a little to maintain—for instance, to check whether the intelligence is still good and whether the implants are still functioning and accessible (and, if not, to replace them). If the number of implants discovered rises precipitously, that increase could be an indicator of accelerated activity leading to conflict, but it might also be a result of an unexpected change in the discovery mechanism (or, conversely, an unexpected degradation in the attacker's ability to conceal implants). Given how rarely implants are found, it may also be a statistical artifact. Might a good indicator of an attack be an acceleration of bulwarking actions as the attacker braces against an expected retaliation? Perhaps, yet many such preparations can be made nearly instantly, by flipping a virtual switch, if planned properly.

Consider what happens, therefore, when a state's preparation level unexpectedly rises. Perhaps the security folks have just won their bureaucratic argument against the laissez-faire folks. System administrators could be reacting to a news item, such as discovery of the Stuxnet worm. Maybe some laboratory demonstration revealed how vulnerable the state's key systems were—or, conversely, how easy it would be to secure them if certain new technologies were employed. But potential adversaries may have no insight into which motivations were present. They might assume that whatever the suddenly better-defended state does is all about them. Thus, they reason, such preparations can only be prefatory to attack. Perhaps a potential adversary attacks first or takes other actions that are interpreted by the presumed soon-to-be attacker in the worst way. Crisis follows.

In cyberspace, as in the physical world, what one state believes is standard operating procedure may be interpreted as anything but by another state. Two factors exacerbate the problem in cyberspace. First, because states constantly penetrate one another's networks, they are in a position to observe many things about target states, but only in partial ways; if they make conclusions about the whole from the part, miscalculation may result. Second, cyberwar is too new and untested for a universal set of standard operating procedures—much less a well-grounded understanding of another state's standard operating procedures—to have evolved.

Finally, a crisis can start over nothing at all. Because preparations for cyberattack are often generally invisible (if they are to work), there is little good evidence that can be offered to prove that one state is *not* starting to attack the other. States may try to assuage fears touched off by otherwise unmemorable incidents by demanding proof that the other side is not starting something. If proof is not forthcoming (and what *would* constitute proof, anyway?), matters could escalate.

Too Much Confidence in Attribution

Inadvertent crises may stem from difficulties in attribution. Take catalytic warfare.[20] Posit a third party, Yellow, that wants a conflict between Red and Blue. Yellow may have been motivated for any number of reasons: (1) either Red or Blue is putting too much pressure on Yellow,

---

[20] William A. Owens, Kenneth W. Dam, and Herbert S. Lin, eds., *Technology, Policy, Law, and Ethics Regarding U.S. Acquisition and Use of Cyberattack Capabilities*, Washington, D.C.: National Academies Press, 2009, Chapter Nine.

(2) Yellow's friendship would become more valuable for Red or Blue if both were at crossed swords and needed allies desperately, (3) Yellow and Blue are competing for Red's attention (or business) and putting Red and Blue at odds can only help Yellow, or (4) if Red and Blue are distracted by one another, Yellow has a freer hand in the rest of the world. Or maybe Yellow is plain mischievous. So, Yellow attacks Red and makes it look like Blue was the attacker. If the gambit works, Red and Blue find themselves in a crisis that neither wanted. If the gambit fails—because Yellow was too optimistic about the difficulties of attribution—it gets blamed. This starts a different crisis that could have been avoided if Yellow's assessment had been correct. Perhaps even Yellow's intent to have one side blame the other is also revealed. So Yellow finds itself in an avoidable crisis with Blue or Red or both.

Misattribution does not have to be direct. Red may attack Blue, which turns around and blames Red's friend Orange—a state deemed more sophisticated at cyberarts—not because Orange did it but because the close working relationship between Red and Orange implicated Orange. Blue figures that Red could not have carried out such an attack itself. Red, for its part, believes that the help it got from Orange was secondary and therefore attacked without considering that such an attack would start a crisis between Orange and Blue. Redirection, as such, is not solely a property of cyberspace, but the problem may be worse in cyberspace because the assistance given between two states is much harder to see. It need involve only an exchange of people, and even that is unnecessary if the relevant assistance can be provided over the wire.[21]

Too Much Confidence in or Fear of Preemption

One stabilizing factor in cybercrises, compared with kinetic or nuclear crises, is that one side cannot disarm another and therefore has no reason to act on its growing nervousness that the other side may be plotting a cyberattack. This logic, however, presumes, that both sides

---

[21] In that respect, assistance for cyberwar operations has parameters similar to intelligence support for military operations, and both may engender the same accusations of unwarranted third-party help.

understand as much, and they may not. Some within the U.S. national security community—whose sophistication in these matters is second to none—still believe that counterforce, and thus preemptive counterforce, has its place. Military cultures that place a larger emphasis on stratagems and preemption (e.g., China's) may well be even more willing to carry out a cyberattack in the hopes that it will make them safer by disarming their foes.

The same logic holds for psychological preemption. States, afraid of cyberwar, may reason that cyberattacks (or particularly brazen acts of system penetration) may warn others away from starting a crisis. Compared with acts of violence, cyberattacks, by being bloodless, supposedly have the advantage that their use will not induce the target to call for revenge and thus set off the crisis that such preemption was meant to quash. This strategy presupposes a middle ground between attacks that are too inconsequential to merit notice and those that are too consequential to merit absorbing without a response, and it presupposes that a given cyberattack, or set of cyberattacks, can actually hit that middle ground.

The reverse of this fear is also destabilizing. One state may believe that another will carry out a cyberattack on its (conventional) armed forces. Fearing that it must use such forces or lose the ability to command them, it launches a war while it still can (by its own estimation).[22] Even setting aside those arguments that suggest the difficulty of using cyberwar to negate effective C2 (which tends to be hardened and redundant), the while-it-still-can argument is a matter of space and time. The logic of space supposes either that launching war either interferes with plans to disrupt C2 (such as moving ships out of port and out to sea)—despite good grounds for believing that moving off to war has much effect on the efficacy of cyberattacks, or at least any more effect than changing IP addresses or routing architectures (neither of which requires going to war). The logic of time supposes that starting operations at once can move the ball far enough before C2

---

[22] Richard Ned Lebow, *Nuclear Crisis Management: A Dangerous Illusion*, Ithaca, N.Y.: Cornell University Press, 1987, argues that preemption and the fear of losing control account for two of the primary factors leading to inadvertent conflict in the nuclear realm.

is lost to cyberattacks. Such reasoning presumes that kinetic military effects are faster than cybermilitary effects. As a general rule, however, although cybereffects can be turned on instantly, they often take a long time to plan. The one form of cyberattack that can be planned and executed quickly—DDOS attacks—have little effect on C2 systems, as explained in Appendix B, unless they, inexplicably, travel over Internet links. If not only the crisis but also the hostility of the adversary is truly a surprise (as it might be if it just took power in an erstwhile friendly state), then cyberattacks are very hard to organize. If the possibility of a crisis and the identity of the adversary are realized beforehand, then a state capable of carrying out cyberattacks may well have laid the groundwork for one long ago. In other words, by the time the crisis hits, the terrain is mined, so to speak. A sudden rise to war has no better chance of evading cyberattacks against C2 than a more leisurely stroll to war. Nevertheless, that the logic of preemption is faulty does not mean that some states will not believe it and act accordingly.

Supposedly Risk-Free Cyberattacks

A state testing the ground for war may start with a cyberattack against its foes. If it works, success on the battlefield may be much more likely, and war starts. If it fails, too few fingerprints would be left behind to permit the target to respond confidently. Possible gain, no pain—what is not to like? But what if such judgments err and the so-called costless cyberattack leads to war?

The target may make attribution based on the cyberevidence at hand (e.g., forensics, deduction from context, or human intelligence on the likely modus operandi of such an attack). Or, the attacker may leave physical clues, such as the sound of tanks rolling to the front. Because the effects of disruptive cyberattacks are usually temporary, the attacker should count on no more than a brief interval in which to exploit confusion. If success in the physical world is contingent on success in the virtual world, and the onset of operations awaits confirmation that the foe's capability has been significantly reduced, the attack window is necessarily shorter to accommodate the time required to attain confirmation.[23] The attacker may have to start rolling before the cyberattack starts. If the cyberattack fails *invisibly*, then the target's prewar intelligence on the potential attacker may be ambiguous; it is unclear why the attacker moved forces to the border or carried out a "training" exercise. However, if the attack fails *visibly*, the hitherto-ambiguous prewar intelligence takes on a new and more sinister coloration—even absent forensic confirmation of attribution. Physical evidence also clarifies the false-flag problem (e.g., was it China, or was it Taiwan trying to make us think that it was China?). So, it turns out that a preliminary cyberattack was not as risk-free as the attacker may have initially thought.

Finally, certain types of cyberattacks virtually beg for their activation irrespective of whatever else is going on at the time. A state may contemplate a prefatory cyberattack on a normally air-gapped system of a target state. The system is vulnerable because of the possibility that someone will transfer a USB drive à la Stuxnet between an infected machine out in the open and a susceptible machine within the air-gapped system. But *activating* such malware at a particular time is difficult if such transfers are occasional. One cannot count on such a transfer to take place within a given interval. The hackers succeed in penetrating the system but then must sheepishly tell their leadership that the only way such an attack might work is if they *preset* it to go off at given time. If the time comes and the attack takes place without a corresponding kinetic action to take advantage of the narrow window of opportunity, the weapon will be to no military effect, but the cyberattackers will not get a second chance because the vulnerabilities and techniques that permitted such an attack would be revealed. The attacker's cybercommunity would have lost its best punch, and the target will learn what cyberdefense mistakes not to make again. The attackers convince their leadership that it would be a pity to see such a weapon wasted. Thus, starting the kinetic attack, irrespective of all other circumstances, is deemed the only sound course of action. Such an attack would thereby not be as risk-free as advertised.

---

[23] If success is undoubted and the drive to the front is already under way, the fact that war started with a cyberattack is beside the point; the conflict is not inadvertent.

Neutrality

A crisis may start or grow more complex because one state believes that neutral states allowed attackers to traverse its territory, in violation of the laws and expectations of neutrality. What makes sense in terms of norms for neutrality, however, are different in cyberspace.

Take border crossing. In the physical world, for instance, belligerents are enjoined from crossing neutral countries to attack one another. Neutral states that allow attacks to cross their borders endanger their neutrality. In cyberspace, however, neutrals may not be able to distinguish enemy forces from all other traffic crossing their territory.[24] After all, if neutral parties could detect such attacks, the target should have been able to detect (and filter) them out as well. Only the target knows what systems it has, their weak parts, and thus what an adversary armed with intelligence on them would go after. Perhaps the neutral (1) was more sophisticated than the target *and* (2) routinely scrubbed malware from traffic that traverses its borders. Even so, would it be obligated to report what it finds, particularly if it would prefer hiding the existence, much less the workings, of such filtering?

Regulating behavior *toward* neutrals is also different in cyberspace. In the physical world, country A is not enjoined from bombing a dual-use factory supplying military parts located in country B, with which it is at war, even if the factory itself is owned by citizens of a neutral country C.[25] Similarly, country A is not enjoined from taking down a server in country B even though it also provides critical services for country C.[26] In practice, the interconnections and cross-dependencies among world's information systems grow harder to trace by the day. The harder they are to trace, the greater the likelihood that any given attack will impinge on what may be (or appear to be) someone's pre-

---

[24] A neutral whose lands are crossed by a fiber optic line that does not go through a local router or switch may be incapable of knowing the existence, much less content, of such packets.

[25] Prudence, however, may dictate forbearance even when there is adequate cause for hostility. The allies, for instance, never delivered a demarche to Sweden in World War II even though Swedish ball bearings are what kept the Wehrmacht moving.

[26] To take but one example, China's air-reservation systems are hosted on U.S.-based computers.

rogatives or property. If that someone is a U.S. citizen, then, at least in the United States, the lawyers will have their say about the legality or at least appropriateness of attacks. Over time, experience will accrete, case law may accumulate, and thus the inhibitions imposed by lawyers are likely to become, if not smaller, then more predictable.

Should some slice of global cyberspace be off-limits to all state attackers? If so, what ensures that no sanctuary hosts a function that would be considered a legitimate war target? Perhaps a blind eye works best. If the United States wants to knock out an overseas web site used for terrorist recruiting, there may be a deal in the making ("we will not blame your country for hosting such a web site if you do not blame us for sending bytes into your country to put it out of commission").[27] Would the United States object, for instance, if one party to a quarrel took down a U.S.-based server that was providing essential services, such as port management, to the other party? Technically, doing so is a violation of U.S. law, but how different is the legality of such an act from U.S. action against the terrorist web site located in a country that regards such speech as protected? Conversely, does the United States want to establish itself as a safe haven for web sites as long as their owners' home nations are on good terms with the United States? If so, is the United States prepared to act against those that carry out such acts on the U.S. homeland, assuming that it knows where exactly the data were sitting? And if that is so, is the United States willing to accept that the right to react to external hackers going after third parties extends to all other states?

Conclusions

Would the advent of cyberwar lead to strategic instability? There are no first-strike advantages, the proper reaction to indications and warnings of use is defensive rather than offensive (two very separate actions), and

---

[27] Host countries are more likely to want to take care of such a web site their way without U.S. help.

arms races in cyberspace are not as meaningful or as damaging as their physical-world counterparts.

However, cyberwar may not be seen as it really is, and states may react out of fear rather than calculation. There are many traditional ways an unwanted crisis can start. Perhaps, an action that looks innocent to one side—a standard operating procedure, as it were—looks menacing to the other. A covert move was discovered and has to be explained. A move with only tactical or commercial implications is viewed through a strategic lens and agitates others. Two suspicious states maneuver to establish their credibility; one begins to obsess that its reputation and resolve have fallen into doubt and must take strong actions to reestablish its capacity to induce caution in others.

Cyberwar, we contend, is heir to all these risks, and more. It engenders worry perhaps inordinately. There is little track record of what it can and cannot do. Attribution is difficult, and the difficulties can tempt some, while the failure to appreciate such difficulties can tempt others. Espionage, crime, and attack look very similar. Nonstate actors can simulate state actors. Everything is done in great secrecy, so what one state does must be inferred and interpreted by others. Fortunately, mistakes in cyberspace do not have the potential for physical catastrophe that mistakes do in the nuclear arena. Unfortunately, that fact may lead people to ignore the roles of uncertainty and doubt in assessing the risk of inadvertent crisis.

Another way of gauging the effect of cyberwar on crisis management is to look at the systemic attributes of a cybercrisis. To generalize, a situation in which there is little pressure to respond quickly, in which a temporary disadvantage or loss is tolerable, and in which there are grounds for giving the other side some benefit of the doubt is one in which there is time for crisis management to work. Conversely, if the failure to respond quickly causes a state's position to erode, a temporary disadvantage or degree of loss is intolerable, and there are no grounds for disputing what happened, who did it, and why—then states may conclude that they must bring matters to a head quickly. Paradoxically, although the facts of cyberoperations suggest that the systemic features of cybercrises lend themselves to resolution, perceptions of cyberoperations may drive participants toward exacerbation.

CHAPTER SIX

Can Cybercrises Be Managed?

Crises are usually best avoided or resolved with speed. Cybercrises are no exception. Perhaps there are times when a lesson needs to be forced on others. Perhaps, someone else wants a crisis for reasons having nothing to do with what any other state (or at least the United States) did, and a response of some sort is, alas, unavoidable. But, often, there are choices that can be made.

Cybercrises are not an inevitable feature of cyberspace per se. Because it is nearly impossible to disarm cyberattackers, and because cyberdefense is rarely utilized to its fullest (e.g., by disconnecting networks), states have many options short of hostility if they sense trouble on the horizon in cyberspace. In the nuclear era, the threat was from the delicate balance of fear, while, in cyberspace, doubt, uncertainty, and the resulting confusion are more salient. This makes real the prospect of a cybercrisis among quarreling states whenever cooler heads do not prevail.

Crises have before and during phases. Many of the same principles that work to moderate or manage politico-military crises beforehand apply to cybercrises as well: Do not present an easy and lucrative target, foster at least a hint of intimidation for those that do not mean well, and look for norms that help in distinguishing aggression that demands a response from behavior that does not. The principles apply differently in cyberspace, of course, a medium in which doubt and uncertainty play much the same role that fear played in the nuclear crises. A state's attempts to demonstrate its ability to defend and attack are not so easy. But the basics are the same.

Similarly, when a state finds itself in a crisis, many of the principles applicable to politico-military crises apply to cybercrises. The management of a crisis is generally best kept in state hands (even if the implied threat that a crisis could gain a life of its own may have a certain deterrent appeal *beforehand*). Hence the importance of a good story for the rest of the world so as to garner support at home and abroad while making it clear to all parties what the principles and the stakes are. Hence, too, the adroit use of dialogue and signals to communicate a state's interest in terminating a crisis on terms it can tolerate. Even if a crisis descends into conflict, the work does not end: Escalation management lies within the realm of the possible and can be used to limit the width and depth of the conflict itself in both the virtual and the physical realms.

Managing crises takes place at the level of the national command authority, and the Air Force follows the guidance it gets. Because the operational control over offense and much of defense is currently vested with USCYBERCOM, the Air Force, institutionally, is limited to its Title 10 responsibilities to organize, train, and equip.

That noted, the Air Force can still do a great deal to assist in cybercrisis management:

- Crisis stability requires that the Air Force find ways of conveying to others that its missions can be carried out in the face of a full-fledged cyberattack, lest adversaries come to believe that a large-scale, no-warning cyberattack can provide a limited but sufficient window of vulnerability to permit kinetic operations.
- The Air Force needs to carefully watch the messages it sends out about its operations, both explicit (e.g., statements) and implicit. To be sure, cyberspace, in contrast to the physical domains, is an indoor and not an outdoor arena. It may thus be hard to predict what others will see about offensive Air Force operations in cyberspace, much less how they might read such operations. But the assumption that unclassified networks are penetrated and thus being read by potential adversaries may be a prudent, if pessimistic, guide to how potential adversaries may make inferences about Air Force capabilities and intentions.

- Assuming that there is a master narrative about any such cyber-crisis, it is necessary that Air Force operations support rather than contradict such a narrative. The Air Force should, in this regard, consider how cyberspace plays in the Air Force's own master narrative as a source of potentially innovative alternatives—wisely selected and harvested—to meet military and national security objectives.
- The Air Force should clearly differentiate cyberwar operations that can be subsumed under kinetic operations from cyberwar operations that cannot be subsumed. Cyberwar operations that can be subsumed under kinetic operations are unlikely to be escalatory (although much depends on how such options are perceived) when their effects are less hazardous than the kinetic alternative would be.[1] Cyberwar operations that cannot be so subsumed, however, may create effects that could not be achieved by kinetic operations that, if undertaken, would be universally perceived as escalatory.
- Finally, Air Force planners need a precise understanding of how their potential adversaries would perceive the escalatory aspect of potential offensive operations. Again, more work, with particular attention to specific foes, is warranted. For this purpose (and for many others), the Air Force would be advised to develop itself as an independent source of expertise on cyberwar.

---

[1] That is, it is probably not escalatory to carry out a cyberattack on a target that one would otherwise hit using kinetic means (e.g., bombs). A potential attacker might think that, because the weapons are cyber, a cyberattack on a target that it would not consider attacking kinetically because a kinetic attack would be escalatory would not be seen as inducing an escalatory response from the target. But the potential attacker might not be correct in making that assumption.

Distributed Denial-of-Service Attacks

Cyberattacks generally succeed because they penetrate and can then give instructions (or corrupted data) to target systems. The systems that are so harmed are the systems that are deceived into accepting and following such instructions. With a DDOS attack, however, the systems that are deceived are not the systems that are harmed. A DDOS attack subverts multiple computers when are they told to flood all routes to a designated target computer in ways that prevent others from contacting the target computer; sometimes, intermediate servers crash as a result.

Thus, well-secured systems can still suffer from DDOS attacks launched from other machines.

DDOS attacks have received a great deal of attention in past years, largely because the primary *political* uses of cyberattacks have been DDOS attacks on Estonia (2007) and Georgia (2008) carried out by Russia or hackers sympathetic to Russian aims. DDOS attacks have also been used against political dissidents.[1] Such attacks have been used to epitomize cyberwarfare in general, with one U.S. military

---

[1] See Bettina Wassener, "Google Links Web Attacks to Vietnam Mine Dispute," *New York Times*, March 31, 2010. In the wake of action against WikiLeaks, a group of anonymous users flooded sites associated with denying financial or hosting services to the site, but such attacks involved the actions of hundreds or thousands of willing participants, not bots (John F. Burns and Ravi Somaiya, "Hackers Attack Those Seen as WikiLeaks Enemies," *New York Times*, December 8, 2010).

officer arguing in favor of creating an army of botnets.[2] The potential horrors associated with unleashing bots controlled by the Conficker worm have been richly described.[3] According to someone close to such deliberations, a DDOS attack coming out of North Korea in 2009 almost persuaded U.S. officials to disconnect South Korea from the U.S. portion of the Internet.

Many of the solutions to U.S. cybercrises specifically address DDOS attacks. For instance, much of the draft-for-comment 2002 "National Strategy to Secure Cyberspace" dwelled on how to get home users to practice safe computing so that their computers could not be used to attack others.[4] The debate over whether ISPs should deny Internet access to users with infected machines, or at least offer them anti-malware protection,[5] grew from concerns about today's information ecology, in which perhaps one of six personal computers is a bot. Those who argue that security is underprovided and that insecure users put others at risk have the DDOS image in mind. Finally, the notion that nations have a responsibility for the bad packets that exit their borders tends to reflect DDOS attacks (in which the unexpected volume of traffic is a sign that some channel should be suppressed) rather than cyberattacks that rely on deception (in which it is hard to distinguish deceptive packets from straightforward ones).

But DDOS attacks are not particularly damaging. They cannot steal or corrupt data; they cannot interfere with the internal operations of networks, notably those that undergird U.S. energy and telecommu-

---

[2] Charles W. Williamson III, "Carpet Bombing in Cyberspace: Why America Needs a Military Botnet," *Armed Forces Journal*, May 2008. See also Stephen W. Korns, "Botnets Outmaneuvered: Georgia's Cyberstrategy Disproves Cyberspace Carpet-Bombing Theory," *Armed Forces Journal*, January 2009.

[3] Mark Bowden, "The Enemy Within," *Atlantic*, June 2010.

[4] George W. Bush, "The National Strategy to Secure Cyberspace," draft for comment, Washington, D.C.: President's Critical Infrastructure Protection Board, September 2002.

[5] In June 2010, an Australian government recommended that ISPs give customers the choice of using antivirus and firewall software or being disconnected (see "Aussie ISPs to Cut Off Unsafe Web Users?" *CNET*, June 23, 2010).

nication infrastructures.[6] The only harm they can do is to make networks *that depend on public access* temporarily unavailable to the public.

Although a network composed of nodes that communicate with each other only through the public Internet can be interfered with, such interference is necessarily temporary and can, in the longer term, be avoided by tunneling links between local-area networks that are connected through the Internet so that the affected routers give priority to their own traffic. The only way that a DDOS attack on an externally facing router of a network can interfere with internal operations is if the router, itself, can generate more packets than the internal node can process, but then the router can be programmed to throttle back on such data flows. At the risk of oversimplification, Figure A.1, with the Internet on the left and the internal network on the right, shows how. If the connections between a network's externally facing

Figure A.1
Configuring Networks to Limit the Damage of Distributed Denial-of-Service Attacks

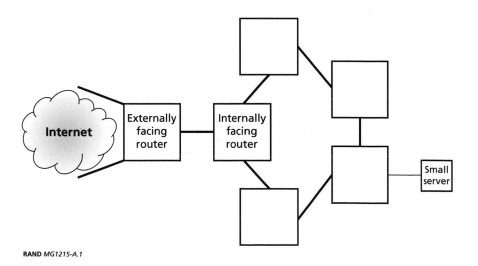

RAND *MG1215-A.1*

---

[6] However, internal networks whose links run over the Internet (because it is less expensive than owning circuits leasing dedicated lines) or whose nodes face the Internet without an upstream incoming flow limiter may be vulnerable to a DDOS attack. No serious infrastructure should be set up this way these days.

router are smaller than the main internal connections associated with the internally facing router, then even filling the former with bytes for the latter will not break the latter or even clog the main connections leading off from the latter. True, if enough traffic passes through the external-internal link targeted at the "small server," then the smaller link to the server itself may get jammed, but only as long as it takes either to crimp the external-internal link or find a way of filtering out traffic to the small server so that the rest of the network has a chance of communicating with the outside. As a rule, however, local-area network capacity is far cheaper than wide-area network capacity, making such conditions rare.

DDOS attacks can often be neutralized. Estonia was vulnerable because its channels to the outside world were relatively thin. Companies, such as Akamai (with nearly 100,000 large web-dedicated routers) and Cisco, redesigned Estonia's network architectures, leaving the nation far less vulnerable after 2007. Georgia's government web sites were knocked out in the early days of its war with Russia. When rehosted on networks operated by Google (growing toward 10 percent of the world's network capacity) and Tulip (a company whose founders had ties to Georgia), they were back on the air and proved far harder to knock out.

Omitting DDOS attacks from discussion allows us to concentrate on the class of more-dangerous attacks that can, in fact, cause a crisis based on serious harm rather than exaggerated harm.[7]

---

[7] Can a DDOS attack take down the Internet by taking down its DNS (the service that converts names in web sites and email addresses to machine locations)? The largest such attack, in February 2007, had a limited effect on the DNS thanks to engineering fixes installed since the previous such attack in October 2002 (Internet Corporation for Assigned Names and Numbers, "Factsheet: Root Server Attack on 6 February 2007," Marina del Rey, Calif., March 1, 2007).

Overt, Obvious, and Covert Cyberattacks and Responses

A systematic approach to attack and response, sorted by the obvious-ness of each, is illustrated in Table B.1.

The purpose of this table is to locate sub-rosa cyberattacks (the lower right-hand corner) within the context of a broader attack-response

Table B.1
Overt, Obvious, and Covert Cyberattacks and Responses

Attack Type	Response Is Overt	Response Is Obvious	Response Is Covert
Overt	An overt response is open cyberwar or at least cyberconfrontation.	Why bother? No one is fooled by the fact that the attacker has not announced itself; everyone knows who attacked.	A covert response puts the onus on the attacker to reveal what happened and explain why. The retaliator may have to answer to the public about why no response followed.
Obvious	The retaliator has to explain attribution in the face of what may be the attacker's denials, as well as the risk of possible error.	No one is fooled by the response, and error is possible. Yet, it lets both sides deny everything if they tacitly agree to settle.	A covert response signals displeasure but also a desire to not let things get out of hand. It may not deter third parties (except via rumor) and will not protect against error.
Covert	The retaliator has to reveal the attack (to mobilize its population, perhaps) and then run the risks of attacker's denial and possibility of error.	Revealing the original attack would justify retaliation, but, if the retaliator is caught, the "you did it too" defense looks contrived.	This is sub-rosa cyberwar. It signals displeasure but also a desire not to let things get out of hand. Third parties know nothing. It may protect against error.

matrix. The attacker has three options: (1) an overt attack (which is noticeable and acknowledged or otherwise of unmistakable origin), (2) an obvious attack (noticeable by the public but not acknowledged by the attacker), and (3) a covert attack (pains are taken not to make its effects public and no claim of responsibility is made).[1] The retaliator, similarly, has three choices: retaliate openly, retaliate in an obvious manner, or retaliate covertly. Note that, over the course of a crisis, the attacker can move from bottom to top and the target can move from right to left but not the reverse: revelation is unidirectional.

If the attack is overt, the target is being dared to respond. It could take the dare openly. It could carry out an obvious cyberattack in response and not take credit, but it could be assigned credit anyway because it, alone, has an obvious motive. It could respond covertly, leaving the original attacker with a choice. The attacker could then reveal the retaliation and perhaps what it was that so irritated the retaliating state. Or the attacker could let retaliation pass without comment and then boast that it attacked with impunity. If the target state retaliates quietly and the original attacker does not let up, the target state will have to answer to its public (and others) about why it did nothing. Its motive for keeping matters covert may be the hope that it can, in fact, persuade the attacker to stop because it will not be obvious to others *why* the attacker stopped; the attacker saves face by not being seen as backing down under the target's pressure.

If the attack is obvious, the target must ask how certain it is of who attacked. Overt or obvious responses present similar considerations. Even with responses to obvious attacks, the logic that the responder is the target of the original attack (or another working on the target's behalf) is supported by the fact that only the target had an obvious motive.[2] The only reason to deny what is otherwise obvious is to permit

---

[1]   The fourth possibility—the attacker takes credit for an attack that it is at pains to hide— makes little sense unless it wants to cover itself in an aura of magic ("we have hit you, but you do not know where and you will not know where until you need the use the system we struck, but, by then, it will be too late"). A major corruption attack may have that character.

[2]   Although there are alternatives: (1) the attacker has struck multiple countries and so the retaliator can be one of several countries; (2) the attacker has multiple enemies, each of which would like a good excuse to strike in cyberspace even if they all have not been struck

both sides to save face while they come to a modus vivendi. Finally, a covert response to an obvious attack signals displeasure but also a desire to not let things get out of hand. It may lead to a tacit or at least covert settlement. The responder could concede that it had been attacked but claim that it had insufficient facts to warrant a counterattack and hope that the target of its counterattack keeps quiet. A covert response will, however, not deter third parties, and it will not protect against error, as explained below.

If the attack is covert, the responder has a deeper dilemma. It can respond overtly in order to make an example of the attacker, which may well deny its culpability and may even demand proof that any such attack, in fact, took place. Such a strategy may be pursued to mobilize public opinion against the attacker, particularly if the original covert cyberattack is a prelude to overt hostilities. An obvious response may be chosen because it permits a wider target list; one need not avoid striking systems whose induced failure would be obvious. If the attacker later reveals the attack, its doing so will suggest to others who the true author of the response is. The risk is that, if the responder is fingered and then claims that it was attacked first, albeit covertly, such an argument will appear contrived.

The purest case is one in which each side attacks the other covertly. The attacker may wish to exert pressure on the target state's leadership without causing a public reaction that may constrain that leadership's ability to respond by cutting back or stopping. The retaliator may wish to discourage further attacks without riling the attacker's public. In other words, each side believes that its public is best kept out of the dialogue. In the event that both sides' leadership consist of hawks afraid that their publics are dovish, they can carry out cyberattacks against each other without undue interference. And so the game goes on until someone concedes either explicitly or tacitly or until one or the other side's attacks are made public. One side could do this itself. Or some action in cyberspace may end up not being as covert as the actor origi-

---

in cyberspace; or (3) the attack gives a third party that may dislike either the attacker or the target an opportunity to weigh in.

nally thought.[3] Alternatively, the exchange may continue indefinitely until target systems have so hardened themselves that attacks are no longer worthwhile.

The retaliator may also wish to limit itself to covert responses because of attribution problems. If it is confident that it knows who the attacker is but cannot or will not provide a convincing rationale to others, then a covert response puts the onus on the target to explain that it is being attacked and why. But a covert response has a sneaky way of indemnifying the retaliator against the consequences of the retaliator's errors. If the retaliator is correct, the attacker will probably have a good idea who hit back because the attacker knows whom it hit, unless the attacker was overly ambitious when selecting the number of states to target. If the retaliator is incorrect, however, the unfortunate victim of retaliation may be left hurt but confused: It does not know about the original attack and therefore has no reason to suspect the retaliator. However, because other evidence may reveal who the retaliator is, a covert response is not risk-free.

---

[3]   According to reporting in *The Epoch Times,*

> [a] documentary . . . meant as praise to the wisdom and judgment of Chinese military strategists, and a typical condemnation of the United States as an implacable aggressor in the cyber-realm [contained] fleeting shots of an apparent China-based cyber-attack [on a server in Alabama that] somehow made their way into the final cut. (Robertson and Zhu, 2011)

The partiality of the source notwithstanding, the actual recording made its way to YouTube. See "Chinese State TV Deletes Video Showing Telltale Signs of PLA's [sic]," *NTD Television,* August 30, 2011.

Can Good Cyberdefenses Discourage Attacks?

Good defenses can limit the damage from cyberattacks and facilitate recovery. They permit states to threaten cyberattacks with less fear of retaliation. The more hopeful case for good defenses is that they discourage others from attacking in the first place (sometimes known as deterrence by denial).

But do they? The answer is complicated and is related to the number of other potential targets this adversary faces, as well as the relative cost of *developing* a cyberattack capability compared with that of *using* a cyberattack capability.

Start by assuming that there is one attacker and one target with perfect defenses. The attacker attempts a series of attacks on one target, gains nothing every time, concludes that it faces no good prospects of success, and decides not to waste its resources trying to attack that target in the future. Here, defense discourages, but is discouragement worth anything? If, having invested in defense (e.g., a fortress wall), the defenders make no further effort beyond routine monitoring (e.g., patrols along the fortress wall) *whether or not an attack is in progress*, then it matters little what effect their efforts had on what attackers do. Indeed, the target is better off having adversaries waste their efforts if the alternative is their investing in something more dangerous. Such logic does not apply to violent conflict, in which it helps to keep the enemy from starting a fight even if its defeat is inevitable: Money and blood will have been spilled.

The opacity and ambiguity of cyberwar suggests that even the consequences of a perfect defense may not be clear-cut to potential attackers. The attacker's decisionmakers will have little direct knowledge of whether or not attacks by other third-party attackers on the purportedly well-defended target are succeeding; all it knows for certain is that there is no visible success yet. Whether *their own* cyberattacks succeed is knowledge that virtually only the cyberwarriors possess. If they persuade their bosses that the right goals—for example, hindering the target's ability to make decisions—have been met but are hard to measure, who would know they failed? They themselves may be discouraged, but, if the raison d'être of the cyberwar bureaucracy were at risk from the delivery of bad news, they may hold their tongues. Without bad news, the attacker's decisionmakers have no way of knowing that their investment is futile. Thus, they are not necessarily discouraged from trying again.

Plausible irrationality may also color the effects that good defenses can have on the willingness to attack. A reasonable attacker may presume that, after so many tries and no successes, the prospects of further success are dim. But it is human to believe that the fault may be not in the difficulty of the target but in the failure to make adequate effort. The more people invest in a problem, the more likely they are to press ahead and try to recoup their losses—the certainty that people can recognize and walk away from sunk costs as such is a conceit of economists, not psychologists. The dynamic nature of cyberspace can convince one that targets that seem impregnable today may be vulnerable tomorrow simply because things change all the time, so keep trying.

Even if we assume perfect rationality, the problem is not so easy. An attack requires three types of resources: general capabilities, such as tools and an understanding of vulnerabilities in commonly used software; intelligence on the structure and vulnerability of a specific set of targets; and man-hours to carry out operations. Assume that all resources go into developing general capabilities (e.g., searching for zero-day vulnerabilities in commonly used operating systems, applications, and hardware devices; understanding failure modes of certain classes of equipment and systems; or building tools that can exploit these vulnerabilities without triggering a target's defenses, such as intrusion-detection monitors or exfiltration filters). Assume also that no serious resources go into monitoring any one target to determine whether a particular vulnerability exists and is accessible (or that such investigation takes place in the course of an attack). Assume further that the attacker has 100 comparable targets. Then one of the targets decides to mount a perfect defense. Does that discourage attack? Not by much. The attacker's prospective gain from investment goes down by 1 percent. If attacks are effortless once the investments are made,[1] the attacker has no reason not to attack such a well-defended target. Indeed, it is hardly worthwhile differentiating the hard targets from the soft targets. Just attack them all. If this sounds bizarre or unusual, it is a fair characterization of the effort required to recruit bots. Botherders generally spend their resources developing or acquiring vulnerabilities and then distributing their malware, such as bad PDF files or corrupted web sites, without regard to who may pick it up. Although the mass use of safe computing practices may discourage such efforts, the efforts of any one user will not discourage attackers, merely limit or eliminate the attack's effects on that user. Herein lies the difference between discouraging investment in developing cyberwar capabilities and discouraging the use of such capabilities.

As a rule, attackers need to invest in intelligence on the target: specific vulnerabilities, standby mechanisms, and the relationship between information and operations in its various systems and commands. It also takes effort to scope targets, carry out, monitor, and provide feedback on an attack. To a large extent, if a large percentage of the effort goes into collecting intelligence on the specific target, then the decision to undertake such an effort depends on the likelihood that such an investment will pay off. Unfortunately, the attackers may have to make target-specific investments to discover that the defenses are daunting. If, at that point, the extra costs of actually carrying out an attack are modest, the attacker may feel that it has little (apart from revealing the target's vulnerabilities to itself) to lose by trying, even if the odds of success are low. If all else fails, hackers will have received live-fire training.

Overall, the greater the role of "generic investment" (e.g., looking for zero-day vulnerabilities rather than target-specific investments,

---

[1] Monitoring targets over time is an aspect of target-specific investment.

such as understanding specific failure modes) in building cyberattack capabilities, the less discouragement a good defense will provide to potential attackers.

Several other considerations merit note. Economic theory says that the greater the price of something, the less people will want it: If potato prices rises, people will eat pasta. If the price of success in cyberwar is high, people will find other ways of hurting their enemies. But the size of the relationship depends on the elasticity of demand. A state committed to achieving an effect, and finding it harder but not impossible to do, may elect to throw more resources at trying.

Conversely, even an imperfect defense may persuade attackers to stop cyberattacks altogether. An attacker may reason that an attempt to harm a computer via cyberattacks will lead to the discovery of the attack and may lead the target to discover how the initial penetration was made. If such penetration techniques are discovered, then CNE—which also requires such penetration—becomes that much harder. The attacker may well refrain from cyberattacks in order to maintain its cyberespionage capability.

But can an attacker, in fact, detect good defenses? If it carried out cyberattacks on a continuous basis—much as cyberespionage is done—then it might detect failure through, say, successively smaller harvests. But it may save cyberattacks for when they might do the most good because it fears that wasted attacks may reveal vulnerabilities and stiffen the target's defenses, If so, its opportunity to detect a good defense may be limited. At best, it can detect increasing difficulties in penetrating systems to spy on them and conclude that cyberattacks are becoming more difficult. However, if the target's defenses are deeper than simple antipenetration devices (e.g., better backup, adroit monitoring, greater overall resiliency), the quality of these defenses may be unseen and therefore irrelevant for their never having been invoked.

None of this says that defenses are pointless, but claims that they may discourage cyberattack attempts need to be viewed cautiously.

Bibliography

Alexander, Keith, "Advance Questions for Lieutenant General Keith Alexander, USA, Nominee for Commander, United States Cyber Command," statement to the U.S. Senate Committee on Armed Services, April 15, 2010. As of June 29, 2011:
http://armed-services.senate.gov/statemnt/2010/04%20April/
Alexander%2004-15-10.pdf

Ambinder, Marc, "Pentagon Wants to Secure Dot-Com Domains of Contractors," *Atlantic*, August 13, 2010. As of June 29, 2011:
http://www.theatlantic.com/politics/archive/2010/08/
pentagon-wants-to-secure-dot-com-domains-of-contractors/61456/

Anthony, Sebastian, "Tens of Millions of HP LaserJet Printers Vulnerable to Remote Hacking," *ExtremeTech*, November 29, 2011. As of July 11, 2012:
http://www.extremetech.com/computing/
106945-tens-of-millions-of-hp-laserjet-printers-vulnerable-to-hacking

"Aussie ISPs to Cut Off Unsafe Web Users?" *CNET*, June 23, 2010. As of July 16, 2012:
http://news.cnet.com/8301-1009_3-20008539-83.html

Axelrod, Robert, *The Evolution of Cooperation*, New York: Basic Books, 1984.

Baker, Stewart, Natalia Filipiak, and Katrina Timlin, *In the Dark: Crucial Industries Confront Cyberattacks*, Santa Clara, Calif.: McAfee and the Center for Strategic and International Studies, 2011. As of April 20, 2011:
http://www.mcafee.com/us/resources/reports/
rp-critical-infrastructure-protection.pdf

Baldor, Lolita C., "US, China to Cooperate More on Cyber Threat," Associated Press, May 8, 2012.

Bar-Siman-Tov, Yaacov, "The Arab-Israeli War of October 1973," in Alexander L. George, ed., *Avoiding War: Problems of Crisis Management*, Boulder, Colo.: Westview Press, 1991, pp. 342–367.

Bhattacharjee, Yudhijit, "Why Does a Remote Town in Romania Have So Many Cyber-Criminals?" *Wired*, February 2011, pp. 82–87, 124.

"Bin Laden Says He Wasn't Behind Attacks," CNN, September 17, 2001. As of July 16, 2012:
http://archives.cnn.com/2001/US/09/16/inv.binladen.denial/index.html

Bipartisan Policy Center, "Cyber ShockWave," c. 2010. As of July 9, 2012:
http://bipartisanpolicy.org/events/cyber2010

Bloomfield, Lincoln P., Jr., "National Security Fundamentals in the Space and Cyber Domains," *High Frontier*, Vol. 7, No. 1, November 2010, pp. 34–38. As of November 23, 2011:
http://www.afspc.af.mil/shared/media/document/AFD-101116-028.pdf

Bowden, Mark, "The Enemy Within," *Atlantic*, June 2010. As of June 29, 2011:
http://www.theatlantic.com/magazine/archive/2010/06/the-enemy-within/8098/

Bracken, Paul, "Strategic War Termination," in Ashton B. Carter, John D. Steinbruner, and Charles A. Zraket, eds., *Managing Nuclear Operations*, Washington, D.C.: Brookings Institution, 1987, pp. 197–214.

Bradsher, Keith, "China Announces Arrests in Hacking Crackdown," *New York Times*, February 8, 2010a. As of July 5, 2012:
http://www.nytimes.com/2010/02/08/world/asia/09hacker.html

———, "Amid Tension, China Blocks Vital Exports to Japan," *New York Times*, September 22, 2010b. As of May 6, 2011:
http://www.nytimes.com/2010/09/23/business/global/23rare.html

"Briefing: Cyberwar," *Economist*, July 3, 2010.

Burns, John F., and Ravi Somaiya, "Hackers Attack Those Seen as WikiLeaks Enemies," *New York Times*, December 8, 2010. As of May 6, 2011:
http://www.nytimes.com/2010/12/09/world/09wiki.html

Bush, George W., "The National Strategy to Secure Cyberspace," draft for comment, Washington, D.C.: President's Critical Infrastructure Protection Board, September 2002.

———, *The National Strategy to Secure Cyberspace*, Washington, D.C.: White House, February 2003. As of July 10, 2012:
http://permanent.access.gpo.gov/lps28730/cyberspace_strategy.pdf

Cartwright, James E., commander, U.S. Strategic Command, statement before the U.S. House of Representatives Committee on Armed Services, March 21, 2007.

Centers for Disease Control and Prevention, "Estimates of Deaths Associated with Seasonal Influenza: United States, 1976–2007," *Morbidity and Mortality Weekly Report*, Vol. 59, No. 33, August 27, 2010, pp. 1057–1062. As of June 29, 2011:
http://www.cdc.gov/mmwr/preview/mmwrhtml/mm5933a1.htm

Cheswick, William R., and Steven M. Bellovin, *Firewalls and Internet Security: Repelling the Wily Hacker*, Reading, Mass.: Addison-Wesley, 1994.

"Chinese State TV Deletes Video Showing Telltale Signs of PLA's [sic]," NTD Television, August 30, 2011. As of July 16, 2012:
http://www.youtube.com/watch?v=fq_jAfiTz-k

Cho, Joohee, "'Obvious' North Korea Sank South Korean Ship," ABC News, May 19, 2010. As of July 16, 2012:
http://abcnews.go.com/International/obvious-north-korea-sank-south-korean-ship/story?id=10685652

Clarke, Richard A., and Robert K. Knake, *Cyber War: The Next Threat to National Security and What to Do About It*, New York: Ecco, 2010.

"Cyber Strikes a 'Civilized' Option: Britain," Agence France-Presse, June 3, 2012.

"Cyber War: Sabotaging the System," *60 Minutes*, June 15, 2010. As of June 29, 2011:
http://www.cbsnews.com/stories/2009/11/06/60minutes/main5555565.shtml

"Cyberwar: The Threat from the Internet," *Economist*, July 3, 2010.

Downs, Erica Strecker, and Phillip C. Saunders, "Legitimacy and the Limits of Nationalism: China and the Diaoyu Islands," *International Security*, Vol. 23, No. 3, Winter 1998–1999, pp. 114–146.

Dunlap, Charles J., Jr., "Perspectives for Cyber Strategists on Law for Cyberwar," *Strategic Studies Quarterly*, Spring 2011, pp. 81–99. As of July 5, 2012:
http://www.au.af.mil/au/ssq/2011/spring/dunlap.pdf

Fackler, Martin, "Japan Asks China to Pay for Damages," *New York Times*, September 26, 2010. As of November 23, 2011:
http://www.nytimes.com/2010/09/27/world/asia/27japan.html

Federal Bureau of Investigation, "FBI, Slovenian and Spanish Police Arrest Mariposa Botnet Creator, Operators," Washington, D.C., July 28, 2010. As of November 23, 2011:
http://www.fbi.gov/news/pressrel/press-releases/fbi-slovenian-and-spanish-police-arrest-mariposa-botnet-creator-operators

Fletcher, Owen, and Jason Dean, "Ballmer Bares China Travails," *Wall Street Journal*, May 26, 2011.

Florida Power and Light, "FPL Announces Preliminary Findings of Outage Investigation," press release, Juno Beach, Fla., February 29, 2008. As of July 11, 2012:
http://www.fpl.com/news/2008/022908.shtml

FPL—*See* Florida Power and Light.

Geer, Daniel, Rebecca Bace, Peter Gutmann, Perry Metzger, Charles P. Pfleeger, John S. Quarterman, and Bruce Schneier, *CyberInsecurity: The Cost of Monopoly— How the Dominance of Microsoft's Products Poses a Risk to Security*, Washington, D.C.: Computer and Communications Industry Association, September 27, 2003.

Gelb, Leslie H., and Richard K. Betts, *The Irony of Vietnam: The System Worked*, Washington, D.C.: Brookings Institution, 1979.

Giesler, Robert, remarks, Center for Strategic and International Studies Global Security Forum 2011, June 8, 2011. As of July 5, 2012:
http://csis.org/files/attachments/110608_gsf_cyber_transcript.pdf

Goodin, Dan, "Crypto Breakthrough Shows Flame Was Designed by World-Class Scientists," *Ars Technica*, June 7, 2012. As of July 11, 2012:
http://arstechnica.com/security/2012/06/flame-crypto-breakthrough/

Gorman, Siobhan, "Electricity Grid in U.S. Penetrated by Spies," *Wall Street Journal*, April 8, 2009, p. 1.

———, "U.S. Plans Cyber Shield for Utilities, Companies," *Wall Street Journal*, July 8, 2010.

———, "U.S. Homes in on China Spying," *Wall Street Journal*, December 13, 2011.

Gorman, Siobhan, and Julian E. Barnes, "Cyber Combat: Act of War," *Wall Street Journal*, May 31, 2011.

Grow, Brian, and Mark Hosenball, "Special Report: In Cyberspy vs. Cyberspy, China Has the Edge," Reuters, April 14, 2011. As of May 4, 2011:
http://www.reuters.com/article/2011/04/14/
china-usa-cyberespionage-idUSN1229719820110414

Hanemann, Thilo, "Chinese FDI in the United States: Q4 2011 Update," Rhodium Group, April 4, 2012. As of July 16, 2012:
http://rhgroup.net/notes/chinese-fdi-in-the-united-states-q4-2011-update

Harris, Shane, "China's Cyber Militia," *National Journal Magazine*, May 31, 2008. As of July 5, 2012:
http://www.nationaljournal.com/magazine/china-s-cyber-militia-20080531

Hoover, J. Nicholas, "Defense Bill Approves Offensive Cyber Warfare," *InformationWeek*, January 5, 2012. As of February 26, 2012:
http://www.informationweek.com/news/government/security/232301351

Hosmer, Stephen T., *The Conflict Over Kosovo: Why Milosevic Decided to Settle When He Did*, Santa Monica, Calif.: RAND Corporation, MR-1351-AF, 2001. As of July 5, 2012:
http://www.rand.org/pubs/monograph_reports/MR1351.html

Howard, Michael, *The Franco-Prussian War: The German Invasion of France, 1870– 1871*, New York: Macmillan, 1962.

"Huawei: The Company That Spooked the World," *Economist*, August 4, 2012. As of August 18, 2012:
http://www.economist.com/node/21559929

Internet Corporation for Assigned Names and Numbers, "Factsheet: Root Server Attack on 6 February 2007," Marina del Rey, Calif., March 1, 2007. As of July 5, 2012:
http://www.icann.org/en/news/announcements/announcement-08mar07-en.htm

Ito, Carlo, "A Brief History of Nefarious Internet Hacking in the Philippines," *SourcingTrust*, March 30, 2011. As of May 4, 2011:
http://sourcingtrustblog.com/2011/03/30/
a-brief-history-of-nefarious-internet-hacking-in-the-philippines/

"Japan and the Broken Supply Chain," *Economist*, April 2, 2011, p. 59.

"Junk Science: Scientists Are Increasingly Worried About the Amount of Debris Orbiting the Earth," *Economist*, August 19, 2010. As of May 6, 2011:
http://www.economist.com/node/16843825

Kaelin, Lee, "Cybersecurity Weaknesses Could Prevent US from Waging War," *Techspot*, November 9, 2011. As of July 5, 2012:
http://www.techspot.com/news/
46190-cybersecurity-weaknesses-could-prevent-us-from-waging-war.html

Kahn, Herman, *On Escalation: Metaphors and Scenarios*, Praeger, 1965.

Katz, Yaakov, "Iran Embarks on $1b. Cyber-Warfare Program," *Jerusalem Post*, December 18, 2011. As of July 5, 2012:
http://www.jpost.com/Defense/Article.aspx?id=249864

Kelly, Meghan, "Cyber Criminals Attack U.S. Chamber of Commerce, China Footing the Blame," *VentureBeat*, December 21, 2011. As of July 5, 2012:
http://venturebeat.com/2011/12/21/china-chamber-of-commerce-hack/

Korns, Stephen W., "Botnets Outmaneuvered: Georgia's Cyberstrategy Disproves Cyberspace Carpet-Bombing Theory," *Armed Forces Journal*, January 2009. As of June 29, 2011:
http://www.armedforcesjournal.com/2009/01/3801084

Lebow, Richard Ned, *Between Peace and War: The Nature of International Crisis*, Baltimore, Md.: Johns Hopkins University Press, 1981.

———, *Nuclear Crisis Management: A Dangerous Illusion*, Ithaca, N.Y.: Cornell University Press, 1987.

Leveson, Nancy, *SafeWare: System Safety and Computers*, Reading, Mass.: Addison-Wesley, 1995.

Leyden, John, "Russian Bookmaker Hackers Jailed for Eight Years," *Register/Enterprise Security*, October 4, 2006. As of June 29, 2011:
http://www.theregister.co.uk/2006/10/04/russian_bookmaker_hackers_jailed/

Libicki, Martin C., *Cyberdeterrence and Cyberwar*, Santa Monica, Calif.: RAND Corporation, MG-877-AF, 2009. As of July 5, 2012:
http://www.rand.org/pubs/monographs/MG877.html

Libicki, Martin C., David C. Gompert, David R. Frelinger, and Raymond Smith, *Byting Back—Regaining Information Superiority Against 21st-Century Insurgents: RAND Counterinsurgency Study—Volume 1*, Santa Monica, Calif.: RAND Corporation, MG-595/1-OSD, 2007. As of July 15, 2011:
http://www.rand.org/pubs/monographs/MG595z1.html

Libicki, Martin C., and James A. Hazlett, "Do We Need an Information Corps?" *Joint Forces Quarterly*, Vol. 2, Autumn 1993, pp. 88–97. As of July 5, 2012:
http://www.dtic.mil/doctrine/jel/jfq_pubs/jfq1302.pdf

Lieggi, Stephanie, "Going Beyond the Stir: The Strategic Realities of China's No-First-Use Policy," Washington, D.C.: Nuclear Threat Initiative, January 1, 2005. As of July 5, 2012:
http://www.nti.org/analysis/articles/realities-chinas-no-first-use-policy/

Markoff, John, "Step Taken to End Impasse Over Cybersecurity Talks," *New York Times*, July 16, 2010. As of July 5, 2012:
http://www.nytimes.com/2010/07/17/world/17cyber.html

Meserve, Jeanne, "Sources: Staged Cyber Attack Reveals Vulnerability in Power Grid," CNN, September 26, 2007. As of July 16, 2012:
http://edition.cnn.com/2007/US/09/26/power.at.risk/index.html

Mills, Elinor, "Web Traffic Redirected to China in Mystery Mix-Up," *CNET*, March 25, 2010. As of July 5, 2012:
http://news.cnet.com/8301-27080_3-20001227-245.html

———, "Expert: Sony Attack May Have Been Multipronged," *CNET*, May 18, 2011. As of May 18, 2011:
http://news.cnet.com/8301-27080_3-20063789-245.html

Montopoli, Brian, "Obama: Malia Asked 'Did You Plug the Hole Yet, Daddy?'" CBS News, May 27, 2010. As of November 23, 2011:
http://www.cbsnews.com/8301-503544_162-20006183-503544.html

Moore, Heidi N., "GE's Jeff Immelt Says It Out Loud About China," *CNNMoney*, July 2, 2010. As of May 6, 2011:
http://finance.fortune.cnn.com/2010/07/02/ges-jeff-immelt-says-it-out-loud-about-china/

Morgan, Forrest E., Karl P. Mueller, Evan S. Medeiros, Kevin L. Pollpeter, and Roger Cliff, *Dangerous Thresholds: Managing Escalation in the 21st Century*, Santa Monica, Calif.: RAND Corporation, MG-614-AF, 2008. As of July 5, 2012:
http://www.rand.org/pubs/monographs/MG614.html

Morris, Chris, "Hackers Take Down Sony's PlayStation Network," CNBC, April 25, 2011. As of April 25, 2011:
http://www.cnbc.com/id/42750388/
Hackers_Take_Down_Sony_s_PlayStation_Network

Mulvenon, James, "Information Warfare and China's Cyber-Warfare Capabilities," speech at Carnegie Endowment for International Peace, Washington, D.C., February 10, 2011.

Musil, Steven, "FBI Seizes Web Hosting Company's Servers," *CNET,* June 21, 2011. As of November 23, 2011:
http://news.cnet.com/8301-1009_3-20073102-83/
fbi-seizes-web-hosting-companys-servers/

Nagaraja, Shishir, and Ross Anderson, *The Snooping Dragon: Social-Malware Surveillance of the Tibetan Movement,* Cambridge, UK: University of Cambridge, Computer Laboratory, Technical Report 746, March 2009. As of July 5, 2012:
http://www.cl.cam.ac.uk/techreports/UCAM-CL-TR-746.pdf

Nakashima, Ellen, "Dismantling of Saudi-CIA Web Site Illustrates Need for Clearer Cyberwar Policies," *Washington Post,* March 19, 2010. As of May 6, 2011:
http://www.washingtonpost.com/wp-dyn/content/article/2010/03/18/
AR2010031805464.html

Obama, Barack, *International Strategy for Cyberspace: Prosperity, Security, and Openness in a Networked World,* Washington, D.C.: White House, May 2011. As of July 5, 2012:
http://www.whitehouse.gov/sites/default/files/rss_viewer/
international_strategy_for_cyberspace.pdf

Ogg, Erica, "PlayStation Network Outage: 6 Days and Counting," *CNET,* April 26, 2011a. As of April 26, 2011:
http://news.cnet.com/8301-31021_3-20057493-260.html

———, "The PlayStation Network Breach (FAQ)," *CNET,* May 3, 2011b. As of May 3, 2011:
http://news.cnet.com/8301-31021_3-20058950-260.html

———, "Sony: PSN Back, but No System Is 100 Percent Secure," *CNET,* May 17, 2011c. As of May 17, 2011:
http://news.cnet.com/8301-31021_3-20063764-260.html

Owens, William A., Kenneth W. Dam, and Herbert S. Lin, eds., *Technology, Policy, Law, and Ethics Regarding U.S. Acquisition and Use of Cyberattack Capabilities,* Washington, D.C.: National Academies Press, 2009. As of June 29, 2011:
http://www.nap.edu/catalog.php?record_id=12651

Parliament of Australia, House Standing Committee on Communications, *Hackers, Fraudsters and Botnets: Tackling the Problem of Cyber Crime—The Report of the Inquiry into Cyber Crime,* Canberra, Australia, June 2010.

Perrow, Charles, *Normal Accidents: Living with High-Risk Technologies*, New Haven, Conn.: Yale University Press, 1999.

Posen, Barry R., "Inadvertent Nuclear War? Escalation and NATO's Northern Flank," *International Security*, Vol. 7, No. 2, Autumn 1982, pp. 28–54.

Public Law 112-81, National Defense Authorization Act for Fiscal Year 2012, December 31, 2011. As of July 9, 2012:
http://www.gpo.gov/fdsys/pkg/PLAW-112publ81/pdf/PLAW-112publ81.pdf

Radia, Kirit, "Iran Blocks U.S. 'Virtual' Embassy Within 12 Hours of Launch," ABC News, December 7, 2011. As of February 26, 2012:
http://abcnews.go.com/blogs/politics/2011/12/
iran-blocks-us-virtual-embassy-within-12-hours-of-launch/

Reagan, Ronald, "Address to the Nation on Defense and National Security," Washington, D.C., March 23, 1983. As of July 5, 2012:
http://www.reagan.utexas.edu/archives/speeches/1983/32383d.htm

Reisinger, Don, "Sony: PSN Difficulties a 'Bump in the Road,'" *CNET*, June 23, 2011. As of June 23, 2011:
http://news.cnet.com/8301-13506_3-20073659-17/
sony-psn-difficulties-a-bump-in-the-road/

Rescorla, Eric, "Is Finding Security Holes a Good Idea?" *IEEE Security and Privacy*, Vol. 3, No. 1, January 2005, pp. 14–19.

Robertson, Matthew, "Chinese Admiral Threatens World War to Protect Iran," *Epoch Times*, December 6, 2011, updated December 22, 2011. As of July 5, 2012:
http://www.theepochtimes.com/n2/china-news/
chinese-admiral-threatens-world-war-to-protect-iran-154434.html

Robertson, Matthew, and Helena Zhu, "Slip-Up in Chinese Military TV Show Reveals More Than Intended: Piece Shows Cyber Warfare Against US Entities," *Epoch Times*, August 21, 2011, last updated April 7, 2012. As of August 31, 2011:
http://www.theepochtimes.com/n2/china-news/
slip-up-in-chinese-military-tv-show-reveals-more-than-intended-60619.html

"Russia Calls for NATO Probe into Iran Cyber Strike," Agence France-Presse, January 26, 2011.

Sanger, David E., *Confront and Conceal: Obama's Secret Wars and Surprising Use of American Power*, New York: Crown Publishers, 2012.

Sanger, David E., and Michael Wines, "China Leader's Limits Come into Focus as U.S. Visit Nears," *New York Times*, January 16, 2011. As of January 17, 2011:
http://www.nytimes.com/2011/01/17/world/asia/17china.htm

Schelling, Thomas C., *The Strategy of Conflict*, Cambridge, Mass.: Harvard University Press, 1960.

———, *Arms and Influence*, New Haven, Conn.: Yale University Press, 1966.

Segal, Adam, "Chinese Responses to the International Strategy for Cyberspace," *Asia Unbound*, May 23, 2011. As of July 16, 2012:
http://blogs.cfr.org/asia/2011/05/23/
chinese-responses-to-the-international-strategy-for-cyberspace/

Slocombe, Walter B., "Preplanned Operations," in Ashton B. Carter, John D. Steinbruner, and Charles A. Zraket, eds., *Managing Nuclear Operations*, Washington, D.C.: Brookings Institution, 1987, pp. 121–141.

Smith, R. Jeffrey, "U.N. Inspectors or Spies? Iraq Data Can Take Many Paths," *Washington Post*, February 16, 1998, p. A01. As of July 5, 2012:
http://www.washingtonpost.com/wp-srv/inatl/longterm/iraq/stories/
analysis021698.htm

Smoke, Richard, *War: Controlling Escalation*, Cambridge, Mass.: Harvard University Press, 1997.

"Sony Laid Off Employees Before Data Breach," Reuters, June 23, 2011. As of July 5, 2012:
http://www.reuters.com/article/2011/06/24/
sony-breach-lawsuit-idUSN1E75M1Y320110624

Stone, Andrea, "Many in Islamic World Doubt Arabs Behind 9/11," *USA Today*, February 27, 2002. As of July 16, 2012:
http://www.usatoday.com/news/sept11/2002/02/27/usat-poll.htm

Suskind, Ron, *The One Percent Doctrine: Deep Inside America's Pursuit of Its Enemies Since 9/11*, New York: Simon and Schuster, 2007.

Tang Lan, "Let Us Join Hands to Make Internet Safe," *China Daily*, February 7, 2012. As of February 26, 2012:
http://www.chinadaily.com.cn/usa/epaper/2012-02-07/content_14551811.htm

Tuchman, Barbara Wertheim, *The Guns of August*, New York: Macmillan, 1962.

U.S. Government Accountability Office, *Defense Department Cyber Efforts: More Detailed Guidance Needed to Ensure Military Services Develop Appropriate Cyberspace Capabilities*, Washington, D.C., GAO-11-421, May 2011. As of July 5, 2012:
http://www.gao.gov/new.items/d11421.pdf

Von Clausewitz, Carl, *On War*, Princeton, N.J.: Princeton University Press, 1989.

"War in the Fifth Domain," *Economist*, July 3, 2010, p. 28. As of July 5, 2012:
http://www.economist.com/node/16478792

Wassener, Bettina, "Google Links Web Attacks to Vietnam Mine Dispute," *New York Times*, March 31, 2010. As of June 29, 2011:
http://www.nytimes.com/2010/04/01/world/asia/01vietnam.html

Waxman, Matthew, "Cyber-Attacks and the Use of Force: Back to the Future of Article 2(4)," *Yale Journal of International Law*, Vol. 36, No. 2, 2011, pp. 421–459. As of July 5, 2012:
http://www.yjil.org/print/volume-36-issue-2/
cyber-attacks-and-the-use-of-force-back-to-the-future-of-article-24

Weightman, Gavin, *Industrial Revolutionaries: The Making of the Modern World 1776–1914*, London: Grove Atlantic, 2009.

Williamson, Charles W., III, "Carpet Bombing in Cyberspace: Why America Needs a Military Botnet," *Armed Forces Journal*, May 2008. As of June 29, 2011:
http://armedforcesjournal.com/2008/05/3375884

Winkler, David Frank, *The Cold War at Sea: High-Seas Confrontation Between the United States and the Soviet Union*, Annapolis, Md.: Naval Institute Press, 2000.

Wohlstetter, Albert, "The Delicate Balance of Terror," *Foreign Affairs*, Vol. 37, No. 2, January 1959, pp. 211–223.

Wohlstetter, Albert, and Richard Brody, "Continuing Control as a Requirement for Deterring," in Ashton B. Carter, John D. Steinbruner, and Charles A. Zraket, eds., *Managing Nuclear Operations*, Washington, D.C.: Brookings Institution, 1987, pp. 142–196.

Wolfe, Tom, *The Painted Word*, New York: Bantam, 1977.

Yong, William, and Robert F. Worth, "Bombings Hit Atomic Experts in Iran Streets," *New York Times*, November 29, 2010. As of June 29, 2011:
http://www.nytimes.com/2010/11/30/world/middleeast/30tehran.html

Zetter, Kim, "Former NSA Director: Countries Spewing Cyberattacks Should Be Held Responsible," *Wired*, July 29, 2010. As of May 10, 2011:
http://www.wired.com/threatlevel/2010/07/hayden-at-blackhat/

———, "Stuxnet Timeline Shows Correlation Among Events," *Wired*, July 11, 2011. As of July 16, 2012:
http://www.wired.com/threatlevel/2011/07/stuxnet-timeline

Zhang, Xiaoming, "China's 1979 War with Vietnam: A Reassessment," *China Quarterly*, Vol. 184, 2005, pp. 851–874.

Zimmerman, Peter D., "Proliferation: Bronze Medal Technology Is Enough," *Orbis*, Vol. 38, No. 1, Winter 1994, p. 67.